1971

This book may be kept

THE REFERENCE SHELF   VOLUME 43 NUMBER 1

ARMS, INDUSTRY AND AMERICA

EDITED BY

KENNETH S. DAVIS

THE H. W. WILSON COMPANY
NEW YORK   1971

THE REFERENCE SHELF

The books in this series contain reprints of articles, excerpts from books, and addresses on current issues and social trends in the United States and other countries. There are six separately bound numbers in each volume, all of which are generally published in the same calendar year. One number is a collection of recent speeches; each of the others is devoted to a single subject and gives background information and discussion from various points of view, concluding with a comprehensive bibliography. Books in the series may be purchased individually or on subscription.

PREFACE

"Almost everything that distinguishes the modern world from earlier centuries is attributable to science."

So wrote Bertrand Russell in *A History of Western Philosophy*—and certainly the basic causal factor, the central developing theme of Western history as process, ever since the early seventeenth century, has been the increasingly strong impact of science and technology upon social, cultural, political, and economic institutions, and upon the individual lives of men. Indeed, it seems not too much to say that every major decisive event of world history for the last two centuries has had as its essence the dynamic relationship (that of challenge-and-response) between man's personal and institutional life and the growing power of his technology.

But is it truly *his* technology? Does he possess it, control it—or does it possess and control him?

The question was by no means merely fanciful in the early nineteenth century when Mary Shelley published her *Frankenstein*. It had become wholly realistic by the early twentieth century when Henry Adams wrote his *Education*. On a November day in 1904, Adams, sailing up New York harbor at the end of a crossing from Europe, saw the "outline of the city" as "frantic." It was as if "power . . .[had] outgrown its servitude" and "asserted its freedom." It was as if "the cylinder had exploded, and thrown great masses of stone and steam against the sky." And when Adams had debarked and was again upon the streets of New York, the city seemed to him to have "the air and movement of hysteria"; its citizens "were crying, in every accent of anger and alarm, that the new forces must at any cost be brought under control."

But they were *not* brought under control, as we now all know to our sorrow. Instead, they continued to grow out of

3

control, distorted into monstrous shapes by the political and economic arrangements of a preindustrial age. They created global interdependencies that were increasingly frustrated by the prevailing system of national sovereignties. They imposed intolerable strains upon social walls and vastly overflowed economic channels that had never been designed to contain them. Inevitably, they heated up under the pressure of their constraint, feeble though this became in proportion to their strength, until, within a decade after Adams had remarked the world-city's cry for their mastery, they did indeed burst the "cylinder" in catastrophic explosion. In July and August 1914, a local quarrel in a remote corner of Europe was sufficient to spark the First World War.

Thereafter, the nominal rulers of the West—the kings, the prime ministers, the President of the United States; the captains of industry and princes of commerce; the generals of armies and admirals of fleets—found themselves the slaves of circumstance; they were helplessly driven by the unforeseen events and requirements of a machine-war which used up living men as if flesh and blood were fuel.

Franklin D. Roosevelt, Assistant Secretary of the Navy during World War I, claimed years later, that the nation's "grand effort" of 1917-18 resulted from "the very remarkable leadership" exercised by Woodrow Wilson and his Cabinet. The "American organization for war," whereby the country's economic power was mobilized and applied to the achievement of a single objective as never before in history, had been "carefully thought out," he asserted. It had been "created *from the top down, not the bottom up,*" he said.

But no one who looks closely at what happened during those years, in historical perspective, is likely to see much evidence of foreknowledge, purposeful intelligence, and executive will as the prime movers, the actual initiators and molders, of stupendous events. On the contrary, one sees a continuation of the process by which the Great War itself came to happen—a process of human inadvertence and machine-compulsion; a process of losing control or failing to gain control over the vast energies which scientific technology was releasing. Far from being imposed "from the top down" by a wise and forceful Executive, the American war organization appears to have been generated "from the bottom up" by the very forces it seemed to organize. Its administrative structure appears the necessary pattern or "natural" shape of these forces when applied to war.

The men who, under the aegis of a Council of National Defense, came to exercise by 1918 a Government dictatorship of the national economy had the means and imperatives for doing so literally thrust upon them—and thrust upon them against their respective wills. For they were all businessmen, or business oriented, ideologically committed to "free enterprise" with a bare minimum of Federal controls. Similarly, with regard to Woodrow Wilson personally and his political Administration in general, a principled, purposeful intelligence was repeatedly overwhelmed or overruled by the events it sought to avert or to control. "In a democracy it is the part of statesmanship to prevent the development of power which overawes the ordinary forces of man," Louis Brandeis once said. And his friend Wilson—the Jeffersonian Democrat, the eloquent advocate of decentralized administration—had thoroughly agreed. Yet under his presidency were heaped up such "mighty Himalayas" (Brandeis' phrase) of concentrated power as had never been before in his native land, and heaped up, moreover, through his own acts—in large part, acts he felt compelled by circumstance to perform.

Nor was there any gain in human control over a rampant and burgeoning technology in the aftermath of World War I. Quite the contrary. Technology advanced by leaps and bounds while controlling intelligence limped farther and farther behind, so that the same forces which had grown beyond human control to produce World War I grew even faster, with even less control, to produce World War II within two short decades. And when the latter war came, America's organization for it was in most important respects a repetition, with refinements made during the interwar years, of her organization in 1917-18. Essentially the same institutional relationships and procedural patterns which had fused Government and industry into an efficient war machine in the earlier crisis were forced upon America to the same end in the latter one. Only the names of the specific agencies were changed.

But this time there *was* a difference—a terrifying difference. Out of the total war of 1939-45 emerged total weapons —weapons capable of destroying all life on Earth within a few hours, and possibly the Earth itself as a physical entity —so that the disparity between destructive power and humane intelligence, in the absence of effective control, was far wider than ever before in all history. In consequence, weapons technology became of itself a dominant ruling force in the world; it determined of itself alone the acts, the thoughts, the feelings of millions of men.

Can or will we conquer this Frankenstein's monster and destroy it before it destroys all of us? This, basically, is the question with which this book as a whole is concerned.

The editor wishes to thank both the authors and the publishers of the following selections for permission to reprint them here.

KENNETH S. DAVIS

February 1971

CONTENTS

PREFACE 3

I. THE RISE OF AMERICAN MILITARISM

Editor's Introduction 11
Fred J. Cook. Militarism Versus Democracy: The Tradi-
    tional American View 12
Sidney Lens. America's Expansionist Elan 17
J. William Fulbright. Our Faith in the Military Is Akin
    to Our Faith in Technology ....
    .... Congressional Record 19
Paul A. C. Koistinen. Arms and Industry: World War I
    and After .... Journal of American History 20
Kenneth S. Davis. The Ordeal of Donald Nelson 42
Fred J. Cook. The Ordeal of Donald Nelson—Continued 58
Sidney Lens. Arms and Industry After World War II ... 61
Richard J. Barnet. Security as Defined by the Military
    Establishment 67
Dwight D. Eisenhower. Memorandum: Scientific and
    Technological Resources as Military Assets 71
Dwight D. Eisenhower. A Presidential Warning ......
    .... Department of State Bulletin 77

II. THE MILITARY-INDUSTRIAL COMPLEX: CRITICAL
    DESCRIPTIONS

Editor's Introduction 81
William Proxmire. The Costs of Military Spending ....
    .... Congressional Record 82
John Kenneth Galbraith. The Making and Makers of
    Bureaucratic Truth 89

Richard J. Barnet. The Managers of National Security   94

Richard F. Kaufman. Military Procurement ....
.... New York Times Magazine   103

Ralph E. Lapp. The Weapons Makers   112

James G. Phillips. Report on Lockheed and the C-5A
Jet .... New Republic   123

Seymour Melman. The Evolution of the New State-
Management   135

Robert L. Heilbroner. The State Within a State: An
Essay on *Pentagon Capitalism*   142

III. In Defense of the Military-Industrial Complex

Editor's Introduction   149

Barry Goldwater. A Reply to Criticism of the Defense
Establishment .... Congressional Record   150

John J. Rhodes. Instant Myths About Defense Programs
.... Vital Speeches of the Day   154

Robert Anderson. The Assault on American Industry
.... Vital Speeches of the Day   160

Ira C. Eaker. Some Concerns About National Security:
Dangerous Times ...... Vital Speeches of the Day   168

Earle G. Wheeler. Will Internal Dissent Destroy National Security? ...... U.S. News & World Report   175

Nathan F. Twining. A Superior Military Technology   184

Anthony Harrigan. Defense Is a Job for Military Professionals .... National Review   186

IV. The Struggle for Control

Editor's Introduction   191

Herbert Scoville and Robert C. Osborn. International
Arms Control Is the Only Answer   192

Murray L. Weidenbaum. A Moderate's Proposals ....
.... Vital Speeches of the Day 195
Ralph E. Lapp. Accurate Information—A Weapon
Against Pentagon Weaponry ...... New Republic 199
James G. Phillips. Taxpayer Suits Against Pentagon
Bureaucrats? .... New Republic 201
John Kenneth Galbraith. Some Ideas for Taming Penta-
gon Power 202
Juan Cameron. The Case for Cutting Defense Spending
.... Fortune 206
Richard J. Barnet. How to Break Up the Military-
Industrial Complex 214
George Wald. We Have Got to Get Rid of Nuclear
Weapons 222

BIBLIOGRAPHY 224

I. THE RISE OF AMERICAN MILITARISM

EDITOR'S INTRODUCTION

"Safety from external danger is the most powerful director of national conduct. Even the ardent love of liberty will, after a time, give way to its dictates. The violent destruction of life and property incident to war, the continual effort and alarm attendant upon a state of continual danger, will compel nations the most attached to liberty to resort for repose and security to institutions which have a tendency to destroy their civil and political rights. To be more safe, they at length become willing to run the risk of being less free."

So wrote Alexander Hamilton in No. 8 of *The Federalist* papers, in 1787, and the "institutions chiefly alluded to," he added, "are *standing armies.*"

"It is said in some quarters that we are not prepared for war. What is meant by being prepared? Is it meant that we are not ready upon brief notice to put a nation in the field, a nation of men trained to arms? Of course we are not ready to do that; and we shall never be in time of peace so long as we retain our present political principles and institutions. . . ."

So said Woodrow Wilson to the Congress in his Annual Message of December 1914.

"America has become a militaristic and aggressive nation. Our massive and swift invasion of the Dominican Republic in 1965, concurrent with the rapid buildup of U.S. military power in Vietnam, constituted an impressive demonstration of America's readiness to execute military contingency plans and to seek military solutions to problems of political disorder and potential Communist threats in the areas of our interest."

So wrote General David M. Shoup, World War II hero, later Commandant of the U.S. Marine Corps, in an article published in the *Atlantic* in 1969.

The contrast between the last quotation and the two earlier ones is vivid. It manifests a change in American attitudes and institutions which the opening section of this book attempts to describe and explain. In the first selection Fred J. Cook describes the antimilitarism of the Founding Fathers, suggesting that the present situation, wherein a huge military establishment absorbs the bulk of the Federal budget, is a complete break with our national traditions. Sidney Lens, author of the second selection, is not so sure of this. America has had from the first an "expansionist élan," he says, and has shown no reluctance to employ armed force in service of it. Nor does the third author, Senator J. William Fulbright, chairman of the Senate Foreign Relations Committee, see the present reliance on military might as a complete departure, a contradiction of our traditional character. He sees it, rather, as an expression of "the American technological bias"—a bias for which we have long been notorious.

The selections which follow these first three set forth chronologically the origin and development of what has come to be known as the "military-industrial complex," the closing selections being an excerpt from President Eisenhower's Farewell to the Nation containing his famous warning against that complex.

MILITARISM VERSUS DEMOCRACY: THE TRADITIONAL AMERICAN VIEW [1]

[It was] one of the most cherished beliefs of the Founding Fathers that a permanent and powerful military caste is the implacable foe of democracy.

[1] From *The Warfare State*, by Fred J. Cook. Macmillan. '62. p 35-9. Reprinted with permission of The Macmillan Company from *The Warfare State* by Fred J. Cook. © by Fred J. Cook, 1962. Mr. Cook is an author and journalist, three times winner of the New York Newspaper Guild's Page One Award while a reporter for the New York *World-Telegram*.

So deep and so widespread was this conviction that one of the major arguments against the adoption of the Constitution in 1787 centered upon its failure flatly to proscribe the maintenance of *any standing army at all*. The great leaders of the day, men of every political complexion, were all genuinely concerned with this issue. They had been reared upon the Greek classics, they had all read their Plutarch, and they were acutely sensitive to the verdict of history—that governments that rely upon the swords of generals for their salvation are in the end themselves sacrificed to the swords of their saviors. Above all else, the fathers of the Constitution were determined that this history should not repeat itself in America, and their concern shines through all their great debates and expresses itself in safeguards that they implanted in the document they drafted.

Thomas Jefferson, studying the draft of the Constitution from his foreign ministry post in France, was shocked by its failure to include a Bill of Rights. Ever the champion of basic freedoms, he argued strenuously for the inclusion of a flat guarantee "without the aid of sophisms for freedom of religion, freedom of the press, protection against standing armies. . . ."

In the Virginia convention on ratification, where the greatest orators and statesmen of the day clashed in the only full-scale debate held in any of the thirteen states, bitter disputes raged about the military powers vested in the new Federal Government. Patrick Henry, leader of the opposition to the Constitution, turned the full powers of his oratory on the dangers inherent in the maintenance of a large standing army. "If Congress shall say that the general welfare requires it, they may keep armies continually on foot . . . ," he declared. "They may billet them on the people at pleasure." This, Henry thought, was "a most dangerous power! Its principles are despotic." He foresaw that "a standing army" would "execute the execrable commands of tyran-

ny." And who, he asked, could resist? "Will your macebearer
be a match for a disciplined regiment?"

Proponents of the Constitution argued that, as long as
there was war in the world, armies would be needed and
any government that was to be created must be entrusted
with authority to raise them. This logic in the end prevailed,
and the Virginia convention ratified the Constitution—but
only, it should be noted, by the narrow margin of ten votes
and only after its advocates had agreed to accept a series of
twenty amendments proposed by its foes. These amendments
were drawn up by George Mason, one of the great Virginians
of his day, and they included the ten that were later adopted
as the Bill of Rights. One of Mason's proposals, approved
by the Virginia convention but later discarded, expressed
the sentiment of the time in these words:

that standing Armys in time of peace are dangerous to liberty,
and therefore ought to be avoided, as far as the circumstances and
Protection of the Community will admit; and that in all Cases,
the Military should be under strict subordination to and governed
by the Civil Power.

This deep concern lest the Military arrogate to itself the
kind of power that ultimately might lead it to dominate the
state was an almost inevitable by-product of the Revolutionary era and Revolutionary ideals. Fresh in the minds of
the Founding Fathers were memories of a Europe that had
been dominated for generations by military castes and had
been plunged into almost incessant wars. Fresh in their
minds, too, was the recollection of the manner in which a
British government that had appeared to them tyrannical
had billeted thousands of professional soldiers, a hostile
army, on the citizens of Boston in the early 1770s, an act that
ultimately ignited the fuse of rebellion. To the men who led
that rebellion and molded the society that came out of it,
the Military was a force that, unless strictly curbed and controlled, would undermine all democratic government.

James Madison, "the father of the Constitution," devoted frequent attention to the theme. In one of his journal-

istic writings in 1792, discussing the more odious forms of government, he denounced first the one

operating by a permanent military force, which at once maintains the government, and is maintained by it; which is at once the cause of burdens on the people, and of submissions in the people to their burdens. Such have been the governments under which human nature has groaned through every age. Such are the governments which still oppress it in almost every country of Europe, the quarter of the globe which calls itself the pattern of civilization, and the pride of humanity.

Again, in his first inaugural address in 1809, with the clouds of the War of 1812 already visible on the horizon, he stated as one of the objectives of his Administration the determination

to keep within the requisite limits a standing military force, always remembering that an armed and trained militia is the finest bulwark of republics—that without standing armies their liberties can never be in danger, nor with large ones safe.

In such statements, the prevailing thought of the time found clear expression, but strikingly enough it remained for Alexander Hamilton, one of the most conservative of the architects of the Constitution, to explore the entire issue of militarism versus democracy to its greatest depth. In several of *The Federalist* essays that did so much to rally public opinion behind the Constitution, Hamilton devoted the full powers of a brilliant intellect to the effort to demonstrate how baseless was the fear that the new government would create a powerful, permanent army. His repeated concentration on this theme is in itself a vivid indication of the importance that was attached to it.

The core of Hamilton's argument was that the new Constitution guarded against the growth of militarism by providing that "the Legislature, not the Executive," should have the power to create an army. In this, he held, the new Constitution followed well-established precedent. He pointed out that only two states, Pennsylvania and North Carolina, had tried to draft constitutional prohibitions against

the creation of military forces. "As standing armies in time
of peace are dangerous to liberty," these constitutions read,
"they ought not to be kept up." Hamilton argued that this
was an admonition, not a prohibition, and he contended
further that New Hampshire, Massachusetts, Delaware and
Maryland had included in their Bills of Rights clauses to
the effect: "Standing armies are dangerous to liberty, and
ought not to be raised or kept up without the consent of
the Legislature."

This reliance on the Legislature to restrain the Military
was the key to the whole problem in Hamilton's view. In
the Legislature, the people's own democratically chosen representatives would control; in fact, he argued, they would
have to control because the Constitution left them no choice.
It contained what Hamilton considered a most important
restriction—a flat prohibition against the appropriation of
money for military purposes for more than two years.

The Legislature of the United States will be *obliged* by this
provision, once at least in every two years [Hamilton wrote] to
deliberate upon the propriety of keeping a military force on foot;
to come to a new resolution on the point; and to declare their
sense of the matter, by a formal vote in the face of their constituents. They are not *at liberty* to invest in the executive department
permanent funds for the support of an army, if they were even
incautious enough to be willing to repose in it so improper a
confidence.

Hamilton supported this factual argument with deep-
probing philosophy. The very isolation of America, protected behind her oceans, made it possible to guard against
the growth of militarism, he thought. He pointed out that
only Great Britain, among the major powers of Europe, had
been able to avoid the evils of a huge standing army and
the dominance of a military caste. This had been possible,
he argued, because Britain's insular position made her relatively safe from sudden, surprise attack, a condition that
would not have obtained had she been a continental power.
Then, in one perceptive paragraph that seems as if it were
written for our own day, Hamilton graphically described

the forces that vitiate and undermine a society not isolated as England and America then were and living in an atmosphere of daily menace that forces it to rely upon the Military.

The perpetual menacings of danger [he wrote] oblige the government to be always prepared to repel it; its armies must be numerous enough for instant defense. The continual necessity for their services enhances the importance of the soldier, and proportionably degrades the condition of the citizen. The military state becomes elevated above the civil. The inhabitants of territories, often the theatre of war, are unavoidably subjected to frequent infringement of their rights, which serve to weaken their sense of those rights; and by degrees the people are brought to consider the soldiery not only as their protectors but as their superiors. The transition from this disposition to that of considering them masters, is neither remote nor difficult; but it is very difficult to prevail upon a people under such impressions to make a bold or effectual resistance to usurpations supported by the military power.

AMERICA'S EXPANSIONIST ELAN [2]

"The Soviet Union," said presidential candidate Richard M. Nixon on October 17, 1968, "is a power still attempting to expand around the world. The United States, on the other hand, is a power whose goal is only peace. We are not attempting to dominate any part of the world; we are merely trying to assure the right of freedom of choice for other nations."

In this eviscerated image the United States seems to have no ambitions that normal nations have, namely the expansion of power and influence; and its Military Establishment seems to have no other purpose but to "resist aggression." We are expected to believe that a society based on private profit sternly subordinates this motive in dealing with foreign countries, and that for the first time in history military bases abroad are no longer an instrument of empire build-

[2] From The Military-Industrial Complex, by Sidney Lens, author, editor, labor union director. Philadelphia. Pilgrim Press. '70. p 16-17. Copyright © 1970 by Sidney Lens. Used by permission.

ing but of helping harassed peoples achieve "self-determination."

If this is true it is a remarkable transformation of a nation whose history is punctuated by an expansionist élan. George Washington referred to the United States as a "rising empire," and most of the Founding Fathers demanded that Canada and the Floridas be incorporated into the United States. "So long as Great Britain shall have Canada, Nova Scotia, and the Floridas, or any of them," John Adams wrote in 1778, "so long will Great Britain be the enemy of the United States. . . ." The War of 1812 was in large measure an effort to achieve this goal. America's eyes were cast west, south, and north throughout the nineteenth century, not only in scores of wars to seize Indian territory, but to seize land belonging to Spain, France, England, and Mexico. "We were guided," said Congressman Robert C. Winthrop of Massachusetts—and repeated by President James K. Polk—by "the right of our manifest destiny to spread over this whole continent." A half century later Theodore Roosevelt denied that the United States "feels any land hunger," but insisted that it had, "however reluctantly" the right to "the exercise of an international police power." We had a right to defend uncivilized states, such as Hawaii or Colombia, "from themselves." Under the principles of "dollar diplomacy" which held sway in the ensuing decades the American colossus no longer sought sovereignty over foreign lands but was content to dominate Latin America through economic and political controls, using intervention only as a final expedient.

To think of the United States, then, as a nation which has suddenly forsworn expansion of its influence overseas clashes harshly with the lessons of history and the theorems of many American military and political leaders. "Commerce follows the flag," said Senator Henry Cabot Lodge way back in 1895. And Captain (later Admiral) Alfred T. Mahan, in his oft-quoted work, *The Influence of Sea Power Upon History,* advocated a large permanent navy to control the seas and expand American trade. With such a navy, said Mahan, the United States would acquire bases around the world, and colonies as a source of raw materials and commerce.

OUR FAITH IN THE MILITARY IS AKIN TO OUR FAITH IN TECHNOLOGY [3]

In the 1830s [the French historian] Alexis de Tocqueville saw America as a nation with a passion for peace, one in which the "principle of equality," which made it possible for a man to improve his status rapidly in civilian life, made it most unlikely that many Americans would ever be drawn to form a professional military caste. . . . Tocqueville was quite right in his judgment that the United States was unlikely to become a militarist society. We have, however, as a result of worldwide involvements and responsibilities, become a great military power, with a vast military establishment that absorbs over half of our Federal budget, profoundly influences the nation's economy, and exercises a gradually expanding influence on public attitudes and policies.

Without becoming militarist in the sense of committing themselves to the military virtues as standards of personal behavior, the American people have nonetheless come to place great—and, in my opinion, excessive—faith in military solutions to political problems. Many Americans have come to regard our Defense Establishment as the heart and soul of our foreign policy, rather than as one of a number of instruments of foreign policy whose effectiveness depends not only on its size and variety but also on the skill, and restraint, with which it is used.

Our faith in the military is akin to our faith in technology. We are a people more comfortable with machines than with intellectual abstractions. The Military Establishment

[3] From "The Cold War in American Life," a speech by Senator J. William Fulbright (Democrat, Arkansas) at the University of North Carolina, Chapel Hill, April 5, 1964. Text from *Congressional Record*. 110(daily):7094. Ap. 7, 64.

is a vast and enormously complex machine, a tribute to the technological genius of the American people; foreign policy is an abstract and esoteric art, widely regarded as a highly specialized occupation of eastern intellectuals, but not truly an American occupation. Our easy reliance on the Military Establishment as the foundation of our foreign policy is not unlike the reliance which we place on automobiles, television, and refrigerators: they work in a predictable and controllable manner, and on the rare occasions when they break down, any good mechanic can put them back in working order.

The trouble with the American technological bias is that it can conceal but not eliminate the ultimate importance of human judgment. Like any other piece of machinery, our Military Establishment can be no better than the judgment of those who control it. In a democracy, control is intended to be exercised by the people and their elected representatives. To a very considerable extent the American people are not now exercising effective control over the armed forces; nor indeed is the Congress, despite its primary constitutional responsibility in this field. Partly because of anxieties about the Cold War, partly because of our natural technological bias, which leads us to place extraordinary faith in the ability of technicians to deal with matters that we ourselves find incomprehensible, and partly because of the vested interests of the military-industrial complex, we are permitting the vast Military Establishment largely to run itself, to determine its own needs, and to tell us what sacrifices are expected of us to sustain the national arsenal of weapons.

ARMS AND INDUSTRY: WORLD WAR I AND AFTER [4]

During World War I, as during World War II, Federal agencies, largely controlled by industry and the military,

[4] From "The 'Industrial-Military Complex' in Historical Perspective: The Interwar Years," by Paul A. C. Koistinen, associate professor, department of history, San Fernando Valley State College. *Journal of American History.* 56:819-39. Mr. '70. Reprinted by permission.

regulated the economy. World War I differed from World War II, however, in that the army, the largest wartime military service, was a reluctant participant in the civilian mobilization agencies. Relatively isolated within the Federal Government and the nation before hostilities, the army was suspicious of, and hostile toward, civilian institutions. It was also unprepared for the enormous wartime responsibilities. Congress and the Wilson Administration had to force the army to integrate its personnel into the War Industries Board (WIB). This integration was essential for coordinating army procurement with the Board's regulatory functions in order to maintain a stable economy.

After the war, Congress authorized the army to plan for procurement and economic mobilization in order to insure its preparation for future hostilities. The navy also joined the planning process. The interwar planning was guided by thousands of industrialists, and by the late 1930s the armed services were not only prepared for wartime operations but also in full agreement with prominent industrial elements on plans for economic mobilization. Those plans, based on World War I mobilization, provided the guidelines for regulating the World War II economy.

Interwar planning was inseparable from defense spending. Many of the businessmen who participated in the planning were associated with firms that were actual or potential military contractors. Despite the relatively small defense budgets of the 1920s and 1930s, the pattern of industrial-military relations during those years foreshadows in many striking ways what developed after World War II.

Mobilization of the Economy During World War I

The American economy was mobilized for World War I by Federal agencies devised and staffed primarily by businessmen. In the Army Appropriations Act of August 1916, Congress provided for a Council of National Defense, which consisted of six Cabinet members, to serve as the President's advisory body on industrial mobilization. It was assisted by a National Defense Advisory Commission (NDAC), composed largely of businessmen serving for a dollar a year or without compensation; most of the members surrendered neither their positions nor incomes as private citizens. When the nation declared war, NDAC assumed responsibility for mobilizing the economy. In July 1917 a more effective mobilization agency, WIB, took over NDAC functions; the former agency, like the latter, was controlled by business elements. Until March 1918, neither NDAC nor WIB had legal authority to enforce its decisions; both were subordinate to the Council of National Defense, and it could only advise the President.

During 1917, businessmen perfected the mobilization agencies and devised the means for curtailing civilian production and converting industry to meet governmental needs. In addition, they developed price, priority, allocation, and other economic controls. By the end of the year, WIB had created the organization and the controls essential for regulating a wartime economy.

Through WIB, industry largely regulated itself during World War I. Key to WIB's operations were major subdivisions called commodity committees, which served under the chairman and his lieutenants. These committees, which made policy for and administered the various industries, were staffed by businessmen who often came from the industries they directed. Assisting the commodity committees were war service committees which were trade associations or councils elected by the national industries. Since the war service committees were neither organized nor financed by the Government, they officially only "advised" the commodity committees. But in practice the commodity committees relied heavily upon industry representatives to formulate and execute all policy decisions.

Even without legal authority to enforce its decisions, WIB had industry's cooperation because businessmen dominated it. Industry's cooperation, however, was not enough to maintain a stable wartime economy. WIB required some control over procurement by the War and Navy departments and other agencies. Throughout 1917 it attempted to coordinate procurement with its own operations in order to prevent the various departments and agencies from competing among themselves and to insure uniform prices and the distribution of contracts according to availability of facilities, resources, and transportation. Economic stability depended upon such coordination, since wartime demand always exceeded supply. With only advisory powers, WIB relied upon the procurement agencies' voluntary cooperation. While most of these proved to be reasonably cooperative, the War Department—the largest, most powerful procurement agency—undermined WIB's regulatory efforts by acting independently and purchasing billions of dollars' worth of munitions. As a result, industrial plants in the Northeast were overloaded with contracts; prices skyrocketed; critical shortages of fuel, power, and raw materials developed; and the railway and shipping systems became hopelessly congested.

The War Department was both unwilling and unable to cooperate with WIB—unwilling, because it feared that the civilian agency would try to take over army procurement functions; unable, because the department could not control its own supply operations, let alone coordinate them with WIB. As many as eight supply bureaus, such as the Quartermaster Corps and the Ordnance Department, purchased independently for the army. Competing with one another and other purchasing agencies, the bureaus let contracts indiscriminately, commandeered facilities without plan, and hoarded supplies. Cooperation between WIB and the War Department was also thwarted by the fact that WIB was organized along commodity lines while the army's supply network was structured by function (such as ordnance and quartermaster). Before army procurement could be coordinated with WIB, the War Department had first to accept the need for cooperating with the civilian mobilization agency and then to centralize its supply network along commodity lines. For months, the department would do neither, not only because it was suspicious of WIB but also because it was torn by internal dissension.

In theory, the War Department was under the centralized control of the Chief of Staff, aided by the General Staff. Serving as the Secretary of War's principal military adviser, the Chief of Staff supervised the entire army, including the supply bureaus as well as the combat troops. This system never worked in practice. The bureaus resisted control by the Chief of Staff. Conflict between the General Staff and the bureaus rent the War Department before the war; it paralyzed the department during hostilities.

Unable to regulate the economy without War Department cooperation, WIB during 1917 sought the authority to impose its will on the department. But Secretary of War Newton D. Baker, reflecting army suspicion of the Board, squelched the efforts to give it more than advisory powers. He managed to do so because he served as chairman of the Council of National Defense, under which WIB functioned, and as Woodrow Wilson's chief adviser on industrial mobilization.

Wilson and the War Industries Board

By the winter of 1917-1918, with WIB stalemated by the War Department and the latter virtually collapsing under burgeoning munitions requirements, the economy had become critically dislocated. The business community and Congress demanded that the crisis should be resolved by placing military procurement under a civilian munitions ministry. Adamantly opposed to such a drastic remedy, Wilson headed off the critics in March 1918 by separating WIB from the Council of National Defense and placing it directly under his control. He granted it broad powers for regulating the economy, including a measure of authority over the procurement agencies. To avoid losing control of procurement and to facilitate coordination with WIB, the War Department also began reforming its supply system. In

December 1917, the department began to consolidate the bureaus into one agency under General Staff control. The new organization was structured to match WIB's commodity committee system.

From March 1918, the strengthened WIB, under the chairmanship of Bernard M. Baruch, effectively used the organization and economic controls developed over the past year to regulate the economy. Procurement was coordinated with WIB activities by integrating War Department representatives and those of the other purchasing agencies into WIB. Once the department reorganized its system and adopted a cooperative attitude, members of the army commodity committees joined WIB committees and shared equally in making decisions. Working together, industrial and military personnel learned that WIB could function for their mutual interests. Through WIB's operations, the foundation for the "industrial-military complex" was laid.

The collaboration of industry and the military continued during the 1920s and 1930s and took the form of procurement and economic planning for future wars. This planning was authorized by Congress in the National Defense Act of 1920, which reorganized the War Department's system of supply and procurement. To insure that the army did not disrupt economic mobilization in a future emergency, the act placed the supply bureaus under an Assistant Secretary of War. It was assumed that he would be an industrialist. The Assistant Secretary would supervise the bureaus and, through planning, prepare them for wartime procurement. Since the Assistant Secretary was made the Chief of Staff's equal, the Secretary of War had two principal advisers instead of one, as had been the case before 1920.

Congress based the legislation upon the recommendations of Assistant Secretary of War Benedict Crowell, various industrial consultants, several bureau chiefs, and other military personnel. Crowell, a Cleveland businessman who had been involved in military procurement since 1916, believed that World War I demonstrated that industrial production was as important to military success as were tactics and strategy. He felt that supply and procurement must receive the same emphasis in War Department affairs as did the traditional military functions. That would not take place, he maintained, under the old system in which the Chief of Staff, aided by the General Staff, served as the Secretary of War's principal adviser. The General Staff would neglect supply and procurement because it knew little about those subjects. Only by placing the bureaus under a qualified civilian who was equal to the chief of staff, he argued, would the army be prepared for future hostilities. Crowell and his associates intended that the Assistant Secretary of War should plan only for army procurement. Congress went further. The National Defense Act empowered the Assistant Secretary, though in an ambiguous way, to plan for an entire wartime economy. Why Congress authorized the more comprehensive planning is obscure.

Establishment of the Office of the Assistant Secretary of War

J. Mayhew Wainwright, the first Assistant Secretary of War under the act, set up an Office of the Assistant Secretary of War (OASW) with personnel drawn from the bureaus. In 1922 an Army-Navy Munitions Board was created in order to include the navy in the planning and to coordinate the supply systems of the two services. And, in 1924 the War Department supply planners organized an Army Industrial College to facilitate their work.

At first, OASW concentrated upon wartime military procurement, but it soon became obvious that this planning was futile without also planning for economic mobilization. Though authorized to draft such plans, War Department officials, civilian and military alike, hesitated to assume what they considered to be civilian responsibilities. It took the influence of Baruch to convince the War Department that economic planning was not exclusively a civilian matter. After World War I, he and other architects of wartime mobilization insisted that the nation's security depended upon constant preparation for war. They favored joint industry-military planning for economic mobilization in order to avoid confusion and delay. Baruch pleaded with the department to draw up full-scale plans for mobilization based on World War I. After years of hesitation, OASW began to plan for economic mobilization as well as procurement. Under Baruch's critical eye, the supply planners between 1929 and 1931 drafted the first official economic blueprint for war—the "Industrial Mobilization Plan" of 1930.

This plan amounted to little more than a proposal for using the methods of World War I to regulate a wartime economy. The key to OASW's blueprint was a War Resources Administration. Comparable to the War Industries Board, the War Resources Administration would rely upon a commodity committee-war service committee system for economic control. The military services would also organize their procurement networks along commodity lines and integrate their personnel into the War Resources Administration. In a future war, the economy would be mobilized by new Federal agencies largely dominated by industrial and military personnel. In 1933, 1936, and 1939, the War Department published revised editions of the plan. With each revision, the proposed mobilization apparatus was simplified and patterned more explicitly after the World War I model.

The fact that the War Department wrote the 1930 plan is of the greatest significance. After ten years of planning, OASW recognized that modern warfare required a totally planned economy; the armed services would have to adapt themselves to the civilian mobilization agencies during hostilities. The Industrial Mobilization Plan did not mean, however, that the army as a whole had accepted the new conditions of warfare. Before that could take place, the supply planners had to convert the Chief of Staff and the General Staff to their point of view. Throughout the 1920s and into the 1930s, the army's command structure refused to recognize that supply and procurement set limits for tactics and strategy; and the General Staff's war plans provided for raising and fielding an army at rates that exceeded the economy's capacity. The General Staff insisted that supply had to adjust to strategy. OASW and the supply bureaus adamantly opposed such thinking. Both the economy and the military mission, they argued, would be threatened. The admonition went unheeded for years.

The General Staff turned a deaf ear to OASW because, knowing little about procurement, it could not gauge the effects of industrialized warfare on the army or the economy and, therefore, continued to view civilian and military responsibilities as if they were unrelated. In addition, the General Staff and OASW were rivals for power. The General Staff resented the 1920 reorganization which deprived it of control of the bureaus. It was intent upon keeping the supply side of the department subordinate to itself. If the General Staff granted the importance of supply and procurement in military affairs, it would strengthen the hand of its rival. Relations between the two groups in the War Department became so embittered in the 1920s that communication broke down almost completely. In the 1930s, however, the strife began to wane. As relations improved, the General Staff gradually became more receptive to OASW ideas.

A Turning Point

A major turning point occurred in 1935-1936, when General Malin Craig became Chief of Staff and Harry W. Woodring, Secretary of War. Woodring, who had served as Assistant Secretary of War from 1933 to 1936, was convinced of the need for practical war plans. Craig agreed. Under their combined influence, the General Staff's Mobilization Plan of 1933 was scrapped and the Protective Mobilization Plan drawn up and perfected between 1936 and 1939. It was the first war plan based on the nation's industrial potential. A radical change had taken place in the thinking of the army's command structure. It had finally accepted army de-

pendence on the civilian economy in order to fulfill the
military mission. . . .

OASW planning naturally led to numerous War Department contacts with the business community. Thousands of
industrialists, most of whom had participated in wartime
mobilization, guided and assisted the department's efforts in
various ways. When the Army Industrial College was organized, it had an Advisory Board graced with such prominent business figures as Baruch, Elbert H. Gary [chairman
of the board of the United States Steel Corporation] and
Walter Gifford [president of the American Telephone and
Telegraph Company]. The various procurement districts
also set up civilian advisory boards composed of army contractors to review the department's supply operations. In
1925 the department organized a Business Council, which
included members from the nation's largest corporations, to
help introduce modern business techniques into army operations and to familiarize the industrialists with army procurement and planning methods.

Most contacts between the War Department and industry involved representatives from trade associations and interested corporation executives. Often these men were or became reserve officers assigned to OASW. By 1931 about 14,000
individuals served in such a capacity. They aided in the
drafting of procurement and mobilization plans and sought
to further cooperative relations between the military and
business.

Mixed motives explain industry's participation in War
Department planning. Firms contracting with the army obviously welcomed the opportunity of working closely with
OASW in order to secure or advance their special interests.
Some business elements assisted the army so that they could
identify their products or materials with national defense in
order to enhance their chances for tariff protection, Government assistance, or other special privileges. Also, their firms
received free publicity of a "patriotic" nature. But reasons
other than immediate economic concerns must be consid-

ered in assessing industry's role in army planning. Industrial preparedness became almost an ideological crusade for some business executives after the war. That was the case with Baruch and his coterie; with Howard E. Coffin, a prominent industrialist and leading participant in wartime mobilization; and with businessmen associated with the American Legion. They participated in army planning as a means of preparing the nation for war. The business community in general was not so disposed. Without being committed to industrial preparedness *per se,* many businessmen were willing to assist in the planning at the War Department's request because it helped the department to adjust its structure and thinking to modern warfare.

The general trend of the interwar political economy is also significant for measuring the response of business to army planning. World War I greatly strengthened the cooperative ethic within the business community and between it and the Government. Before World War II, both business and the Government experimented with official and unofficial attempts at economic control through industrial cooperation. The National Recovery Administration was only the most formal example. The army's economic planning accurately reflected this cooperative trend. (The War Department's participation in NRA resulted directly from OASW planning.) For that reason, among others, the planning received the endorsement of interested businessmen.

OASW did not confine itself simply to planning for industrial mobilization. It also sought legislative authority for implementing the Industrial Mobilization Plan in an emergency.

The Role of the American Legion

During the 1920s the department's drive for industrial preparedness was carried on in conjunction with the American Legion. The Legion rank and file seethed with resentment about alleged wartime profiteering and the unequal burden shouldered by the fighting forces. In order to remove the promise of riches as an inducement to war and to dis-

tribute the burdens of warfare more equitably, the returning veterans demanded a total draft of manpower and capital in any future emergency. Ironically, the Legion's peace
movement, which originated in dissent over the economics
of World War I, was ultimately converted into support for
the Industrial Mobilization Plan based on the wartime
model. Legion leadership and its special relationship with
the War Department explains why. Substantial business
elements and former military officers dominated Legion affairs; throughout the 1920s the secretaries and assistant secretaries of war were usually active Legionnaires. When acting on the proposal for a total draft that was favored by the
rank and file, the Legion leaders turned to the War Department for assistance. In 1922, OASW drafted for the Legion
a bill that in general terms would have granted the President almost unlimited authority over the nation's human
and economic resources in the event of war. The Legion
consistently referred to the bill as a "universal draft," as a
measure for promoting peace, and as a proposal for "equalizing wartime burdens." That was scarcely the case. The
bill was so vague that it could be used for many different
purposes. Its grant of authority was so great and its power
so general that it could sanction a presidential dictatorship.
Once the economic planning of OASW was fully underway,
the War Department and the Legion leadership clearly intended the bill to be a general grant of authority for implementing the Industrial Mobilization Plan.

Beginning in 1922, the Legion-sponsored bill was repeatedly introduced in Congress. Despite Legion lobbying
and War Department support, each Congress sidetracked
the proposed legislation. Unable to get its bill through Congress, the Legion asked for a bipartisan commission to study
and recommend policies for industrial mobilization. An
active campaign by congressmen who were also Legionnaires
soon led to action. By a joint resolution in June 1930, Congress created the War Policies Commission (WPC), which
consisted of eight congressmen and six Cabinet members.

Six of the fourteen commissioners were Legionnaires. The
commission was to study and make recommendations for
equalizing war burdens and preventing war profiteering,
and it was to formulate "policies to be pursued in event of
war."

WPC, like the Legion's drive for a "universal draft,"
quickly became a means for furthering military preparation.
Because the War Department dominated the proceedings,
WPC emphasized how to mobilize the economy for war and
not how to equalize war burdens and eliminate war profits.
Secretary of War Patrick J. Hurley, an active Legionnaire,
served as WPC's chairman. WPC's staff came almost exclusively from the War Department. The department's presen-
tation of its 1930 Industrial Mobilization Plan and Baruch's
testimony on the economics of World War I were the high-
lights of WPC's public hearings. After extended delibera-
tions, WPC, with only one dissenting vote, directly endorsed
the department's planning and indirectly endorsed the Industrial Mobilization Plan. WPC efforts were more impressive as an attempt to popularize and legitimize department
planning than as a serious study of wartime economics.

Despite a friendly commission, the department was unable to drum up much overt support for its plans. In addition to the department itself, the principal advocates of the
planning before WPC were the American Legion and some
wartime mobilization leaders like Baruch, Gifford, and
Coffin. The business community in general was either un-
concerned about or unwilling to commit itself publicly on
issues involving economic mobilization. Of the thousands
of businessmen participating in the army planning, only a
few came forward to testify.

The Opposition

Although support for department planning was weak,
the opposition was vociferous. Witnesses like Norman
Thomas, several congressmen, and spokesmen for some peace
societies and humanitarian groups were hostile to WPC and

the department's plans. Some advocates of peace detected inherent dangers in the department's work. According to their analyses, the promise of wartime riches, while not a major cause of war, was a contributing one that had to be eliminated. The army's plans would not do this. Moreover, the opponents feared that the industrial-military ties resulting from department planning could endanger the nation's future. But the critics—among them a member of WPC, Representative Ross A. Collins [Democrat] of Mississippi—were weak on analysis. Their critique of the department's plans and planning was often nebulous, contradictory, or incomplete. Seymour Waldman, a journalist covering the hearings, articulated more clearly and precisely what appeared to alarm Collins and some witnesses before WPC:

> The hearings revealed a gigantic machine, whose intricate parts touch the entire nation, which is being constructed by the War Department and industrial magnates for use in the event of war. . . . They reveal the dangers inherent in a militarization of industry, an industrialization of the military forces, or a combination of the two. . . .
> [What is needed is a] diagnosis of the whole problem, a study of the interlocking of our war mechanism and our economic system. . . . Such a work . . . is imperative if we are to be effective in preventing more national and international bloodshed.

Opposition to the department's plans and proposed legislation for implementing them increased after WPC's hearings as the peace and isolationist movement gained in strength. The most formidable challenge came from the Senate's so-called Nye committee. In addition to the munitions makers, the Nye committee's purview included economic mobilization for World War I, interwar military procurement policies, and the Industrial Mobilization Plan. In a fragmentary manner, the committee disclosed the dynamics of an emerging "industrial-military complex." The elements were presented in the committee hearings and reports, but they were not fitted together. Senator Gerald P. Nye [Republican, North Dakota] and his colleagues still saw only through a glass darkly. (The Nye Committee findings, although not all of its recommendations, received the unanimous endorsement of all members.)

The Nye committee clearly perceived that industrialized warfare created qualitatively new and ominous problems for the nation. To fight a modern war, even to prepare for one, eroded the barriers between private and public, civilian and military institutions. The committee observed that during hostilities "[p]ractically every important industry in the country is necessary for the supply of the armed forces." "[E]ven in time of peace," the committee reported, "the line of demarkation between the munitions industry and other industries is not clear and fixed."

From its investigation of interwar defense spending, the committee established that various industries depended upon military contracts for profitable operations and that the military services depended upon them for developing and producing weapons. There were many prime examples. Shipbuilding indirectly included "the steel companies, the electrical manufacturing groups, the boiler producers, the instrument people," and "the biggest banking interests in the nation." DuPont and other munitions producers were virtual adjuncts of the War Department. Industrialists and military leaders regarded their interests as mutual. Industry favored and worked for increased military appropriations; the armed services granted industry special favors, encouraged monopoly where it served their interests, financed research, and, despite legislation to the contrary, displayed little concern about profit restraints. Committee members were shocked to find that the War and Navy departments, and even the Commerce and State departments at times, cooperated with munitions firms in a manner that compromised national policies for disarmament, arms limitation, arms sales, and arms embargoes. The fact that Public Works Administration funds, intended to stimulate industrial recovery, went to the armed services and that some businessmen favored defense spending as an antidote to the depression also disturbed Nye and his colleagues.

Employment of Retired Officers

The Nye committee found a web of personal as well as contractual ties binding industrial-military elements. Retired army and navy officers often joined firms contracting with the services. Frequently, officials of corporations supplying the armed services became reserve officers. A society like the Army Ordnance Association, organized in 1919, combined in its membership actual or potential military contractors and retired and active army officers. The Association lobbied for the army, participated in the industrial mobilization planning, and attempted to influence War Department policies and the selection and promotion of personnel. (Concern existed about military contractors employing retired officers before World War I.)

The Nye committee carefully avoided charges of conspiracy. It pointed out that plausible reasons existed for what was done and stated that it was not drawing a one-to-one correlation between expenditures for defense and the causation of war. Nevertheless, argued the committee,

any close associations between munitions and supply companies . . . and the service departments . . . , of the kind that existed in Germany before the World War, constitutes an unhealthy alliance in that it brings into being a self-interested political power which operates in the name of patriotism and satisfies interests which are, in large part, purely selfish, and that such associations are an inevitable part of militarism, and are to be avoided in peacetime at all costs.

In order to check the growth of an "unhealthy alliance," a majority of the committee favored nationalizing the munitions facilities. Congress never seriously considered the proposal. Upon the advice of the Roosevelt Administration, Congress even refused to strengthen regulations governing military procurement as the committee minority recommended.

The army's economic planning for war also disturbed the Nye committee. The planning, argued the committee, assured that industry and the military would function more effectively as a team than they had in World War I; but, because the Industrial Mobilization Plan was patterned after wartime methods, it would not eliminate the "economic evils of war." According to the committee's analysis, World War I mobilization was accompanied by "shameless profiteering" and extravagant waste. The war left a legacy of inflation, debt, and increased concentration of economic power. Similar results would occur in a future war if industry, in conjunction with the armed services, virtually regulated itself. (The Nye Committee was less critical of World War I military procurement practices than an earlier investigation by the so-called Graham Committee.)

In order to secure the nation's economic future and to remove the promise of riches as an inducement to war, the Nye committee maintained that wartime "economic evils" had to be eliminated. That required radical changes in the economic system during hostilities, not the preservation of the status quo as proposed by the Industrial Mobilization Plan. The profit motive and the prerogatives of private property would have to be modified. To accomplish that purpose, the committee supported legislation drafted under the direction of John T. Flynn. In an emergency, profits would be limited to 3 per cent and personal annual income to $10,000. No individual with direct or indirect interests in an industry could serve in a government capacity involving that industry. Moreover, the President would be granted vast authority over the economy to the point of conscripting capital and management if necessary. Although vague at many points, the Flynn legislation amounted to a proposal for state capitalism during wartime with the industrial managers removed from the seats of power.

The Nye Committee and the War Department

The War Department opposed the Committee's major recommendations. It viewed with alarm any taxation proposals that threatened production. It maintained that conscripting management would not work and insisted that

economic mobilization was impossible without the assistance
of managers of the industries to be regulated. Baruch responded to the proposed bill with undisguised hostility. Attempting to change the economic system during a war, he
argued, was an invitation to disaster.

In its most impressive reports, the Nye committee curiously agreed with both the War Department and Baruch.
The Committee's support of the Flynn proposals ignored its
own findings. Without constitutional amendments that
could be "far worse than the situation of profiteering in a
national emergency," the Flynn legislation could not be enforced. The Committee recognized that, even if the bill and
the necessary amendments were adopted, they would probably be repealed or ignored in an emergency. The only men
qualified to administer a wartime economy were industrialists themselves. It was inconceivable that they would attempt
to enforce laws they considered detrimental to the economy
and to the war effort.

The Flynn bill was introduced into Congress in 1935.
For a time, Franklin D. Roosevelt seemed disposed toward
the bill. Ultimately, he joined Baruch, the War Department,
and, with reservations, the Legion in backing competing
legislation that would have granted the President authority
for mobilizing the economy, but with few safeguards against
abuse. That bill would have sanctioned what the Industrial
Mobilization Plan proposed. The Administration let it be
known that it, too, believed that curtailing the profit motive
during a war would jeopardize any mobilization program.
No legislation was passed.

After the Nye committee investigation, the nation knew
more about the political economy of warfare; but short of
avoiding war and excessive spending for defense, there was
no viable way to prevent close and compromising relations
between business and the armed services. Military spending
in the American industrial system inevitably drew industrial
and military elements together, and the threat of an "unhealthy alliance" was always present.

War Department planning entered its final and most important phase after the Nye committee investigation. With the approach of war and the growing American preparedness movement, the department launched a drive for the appointment of a joint industry-military board to review and ultimately to implement the Industrial Mobilization Plan.

The proposal for a joint board originated with civilians who were concerned about a major flaw in the Industrial Mobilization Plan. Because of a continuing distrust of civilian institutions, the army determined to dominate the wartime mobilization agencies. To insure that OASW plans were realistic and to keep the nation ready for war, Baruch and others repeatedly recommended that industrialists officially meet each year with the War Department. They would review the department's plans and prepare themselves for the eventuality of official duty.

The War Department resisted suggestions for officially sharing its planning authority with industrialists until Louis Johnson, a past American Legion commander, became Assistant Secretary of War in June 1937. With international relations deteriorating, Johnson was determined to prepare both the army and the nation for war. He arranged for Baruch, some former WIB members, and younger talent to serve as an advisory board to OASW. For Johnson, that was the first essential step for instituting the Industrial Mobilization Plan. But the President refused to sanction the scheme. Despite the setback, Johnson was determined to create an advisory board. He was stealthily maneuvering to achieve that end in mid-1939, when Roosevelt, fearing that war was imminent and that the nation might become involved, authorized Johnson to set up a mobilization advisory group called the War Resources Board (WRB). Roosevelt chose Edward R. Stettinius, Jr., of the United States Steel Corporation as chairman and left the selection of other members to the War Department. With Stettinius serving as an intermediary, Johnson, Acting Secretary of the Navy Charles

Edison, Army Chief of Staff George Marshall, and two senior members of OASW selected the others. In addition to Stettinius, WRB included Gifford, president of American Telephone and Telegraph; John Lee Pratt of General Motors Corporation; Robert E. Wood, chairman of Sears, Roebuck and Company; Karl T. Compton of the Massachusetts Institute of Technology; and Harold G. Moulton, president of the Brookings Institution. The membership was cleared with the President. Why Baruch was excluded is still unclear. He was described as being "sore as hell" about being passed over. WRB did not get his blessing until his close associate, John Hancock, was appointed to it in September. Hancock played a prominent role in WRB proceedings.

The War Resources Board and the Industrial Mobilization Plan

Assistant Secretary of War Johnson announced to the nation that WRB would review the Industrial Mobilization Plan of 1939, revise it if necessary, and implement it in an emergency. Key to the plan was the War Resources Administration, organized along commodity committee-war-service committee lines with military representatives integrated into it. Unlike earlier plans, the 1939 edition moderated proposed military influence in the civilian agencies.

Working hand in hand with the armed services, WRB, while still reviewing the Industrial Mobilization Plan, began preparing to institute it. In sharp contrast to its attitude toward WPC, the business community was eager to cooperate with WRB. The National Association of Manufacturers and the United States Chamber of Commerce rushed forward to volunteer their services. Through conferences with these organizations, former WIB members, the Commerce Department, and other private and public sources, WRB drew up an industrial who's who to staff the War Resources Administration and also made provisions for the use of war service committees. The most daring move was a memorandum drafted for the President's signature that would have granted the WRB and the Army-Navy Munitions Board authority to mobilize the economy and that instructed all Government agencies to cooperate with those two boards.

Roosevelt suddenly cut the ground from under WRB shortly after its creation because the war scare had waned and because of widespread opposition within the Administration and the nation to it. Liberal Democrats were aghast at the dominant position held by the major banking and industrial interests in WRB. They identified Stettinius, Gifford, and Pratt with J. P. Morgan. The anti-Morgan banking elements on Wall Street who were sympathetic to the Administration were bitterly disappointed. Labor and agriculture were irate over their exclusion.

The President waited until WRB had completed reviewing the Industrial Mobilization Plan and had submitted a final report in November 1939 before dismissing it. In its final report, WRB indirectly endorsed the War Department plan and fully accepted its basic assumptions. A wartime economy should be regulated by Federal agencies largely controlled by industry and the military services. In circumscribed terms, WRB recommended the suspension of the antitrust laws and also suggested that domestic reform would be a casualty of a mobilized economy. It further proposed that the Army-Navy Munitions Board, through consultation with industry, continue to explore the yet unresolved issues of industrial mobilization. It concluded by offering its advisory services for the future. (The ANMB was reorganized and strengthened in 1931-1932, and the Industrial Mobilization Plan was published by ANMB even though OASW continued to do most of the work.) Roosevelt thanked WRB members and never called on them again.

The Transitional Period

WRB's fate did not negate the years of planning. Because of this planning, the War Department adjusted to emergency conditions during World War II with relative ease. In the late 1930s the department began a gradual transition from planning for, to participating in, a mobilization program. Starting in 1937-1938, Congress, after years of departmental advocacy, authorized educational orders and the stockpiling of essential and strategic raw materials and slowly modified peacetime restraints on military contracting. (Educational orders were intended to help industry and the army through the transitional phase from planning to mobilizing for war. Without the restrictions of competitive bidding, the army could award contracts to selected firms for the limited production of various munitions items. In that way, industry accumulated the tools and worked out the techniques for quantity production and the army tested its munitions designs and procurement plans. Educational orders were first introduced before World War I at the instigation of businessmen and public officials striving to prepare the nation for hostilities. For years after the war, Congress rejected bills authorizing educational orders. Before such legislation was passed in the late 1930s, however, the army interpreted the laws and regulations governing procurement in a way that allowed it to grant some educational orders to selected firms. During the 1930s, the businessmen in the Army Ordnance Association launched a drive for educational orders to help stimulate industrial recovery.) As the army and military budgets grew, OASW expanded its staff and activities proportionately until the mobilization stage was reached in 1940-1941. Writing in mid-1940, Assistant Secretary of War Johnson observed: "Without the benefit of plans perfected by twenty years of study the successful and timely execution of this [expanded munitions] program would have been virtually impossible."

When the War Department began the transition to mobilization in 1937-1938, it also launched the drive for implementing the Industrial Mobilization Plan; it had been convinced by the years of planning that civilian mobilization agencies were essential for fulfilling the military mission. During 1940-1941, the Army-Navy Munitions Board played a more active role in mobilizing the economy than the army plans had envisaged. But that was the case principally because the civilian agencies were weak. After WRB's demise, the Roosevelt Administration relied upon the resuscitated NDAC and other agencies that were totally inadequate for mobilization. War Department officials were in the vanguard of those working for more effective civilian agencies until the creation in early 1942 of the War Production Board.

Throughout the years 1940-1941, the War Department, and the Navy Department as well, sided with industry on most major policies involving economic mobilization. After war was declared, the nation's largest corporations and the armed forces ultimately dominated the War Production Board through an alliance of mutual interests. Though officially rejected in 1939, the principal proposals concurred in by WRB and the military were adopted during World War II. As foreseen by the Nye committee and others, relations between the business community and the armed services during World War I and the interwar period prepared the way for the full-blown "industrial-military complex" of World War II and the Cold War years.

THE ORDEAL OF DONALD NELSON [5]

[In May 1941, as France was being crushed by Hitler's Germany in the ninth month of World War II, Donald Nelson, executive vice president of Sears, Roebuck and Company was called to Washington D.C. by the Roosevelt Administration to facilitate procurement of desperately needed American war matériel by the Allies. He stayed on in key posts in the National Defense Advisory Commission (NDAC) and its successor, the Office of Production Management (OPM), as the Administration was forced step by step toward full-scale economic organization for war. He became executive director of a Supplies, Priorities, and Al-

[5] From *Experience of War: The United States in World War II*, by Kenneth S. Davis, historian and biographer. Doubleday. '65. p 172-9, 518-22. Copyright © 1965 by Kenneth S. Davis. Reprinted by permission of Doubleday & Company, Inc.

location Board (SPAB) when this was superimposed by the President upon a faltering OPM, in August 1941. Finally, on January 13, 1942, five weeks after Pearl Harbor, the President concentrated authority over the American war economy in a single agency, the War Production Board (WPB), and named Donald Nelson its chairman.—Ed.]

Next morning, listening to the radio as he shaves, Nelson finds himself and his appointment to be the top news of the day. He hears himself described as "the man who has to tackle the biggest job in all history," and it gives him a sinking feeling. (". . . I had a deeper feeling of humility than I had ever experienced," he will later say.) He also hears himself described as "arms czar" and "dictator of the economy," and this stimulates thought about the general strategy as well as the immediate tactics of the economic war he must command.

It is clear that the economy must be socialized to a degree never before contemplated seriously by responsible Government officials. The distinctions between private and public enterprise must be, for the time being, much reduced, virtually all economic enterprise becoming public to the extent that its energies can be harnessed to the single overriding national purpose of victory in war. The year 1941 has seen the gathering together in usable form of most of the hard data, the accurate and vastly detailed economic information, on which realistic plans can be based. Now the plans must be boldly and firmly shaped. The year has also witnessed the devising and initial testing of most of the Government controls needed for the achievement of planned goals: priority ratings, materials allocations, consumer rationing, price and rent controls, confiscatory taxation of "excess profits." Now these controls must be extended and rigorously applied in every segment of the economy. Full rein must be given the American genius for large-scale organization and administration, for mass production and mass distribution—a genius whose expression in practice has long ago rendered obsolete much of the "rugged individualism" in which most Americans *believe* they believe—but the guiding rein and driving whip must now be firmly in Government hands.

All this may seem to constitute, of itself alone, a radical departure from what most American businessmen are fond of calling "The American Way." Donald Nelson does not see it so. It may *become* a radical departure. Of this he is well aware. And if it is permitted to do so—if it changes the very roots of the American society—then of course the character of that society as a whole will be greatly and permanently altered. The event, however, is by no means inevitable. Everything depends on *how* the vast, intricate job is done, and Nelson's conviction is that it can and must be accomplished "within the framework of the American tradition." The war challenges us, says he, "to prove, once and for all, that our system of political and economic freedom is in fact more efficient, more productive, more able to respond to the demands of a great emergency than the dictatorial system of our enemies."

In this connection he has been often reminded, and will be often reminded in the future, of a conversation he had with Roosevelt in the late autumn of 1940. To be strictly accurate, it wasn't a conversation but an hour-long Rooseveltian monologue—a barrier of talk put up by the President against the resignation from NDAC (and the arguments for resigning) which Nelson had come to the Oval Study prepared to present. The most memorable part of this monologue had to do with Soviet-American relations. Roosevelt told of talking with a Soviet official who came to him in 1933 with a plea for diplomatic recognition of the U.S.S.R. by the United States. [Recognition was formally announced on November 17, 1933, after much haggling over terms—Ed.] The President had pointed out half-jokingly that, since Russia was a socialist state and the U.S. a capitalistic democracy, there seemed to be no harmony of interests between them. The Russian had countered by saying that, as time went on, the actual difference between the systems of the two countries was steadily reduced. "A few years ago we were 100 per cent communistic and your country was 100 per cent capitalistic," said the Russian. "Now we are 80 per cent communistic and you are only 80 per cent capitalistic. A few years hence we shall be 60 per cent communistic; you will be 60 per cent capitalistic, and when that time comes we won't be so far apart!"

But for Roosevelt as for Nelson, the 40 per cent difference that will yet remain, should the Russian's prediction come true, will continue to be crucial if there lies within it the issue of human rights and freedoms vs. totalitarian dictatorship. And this, of course, as Nelson sees it, is the essential issue of the present war. Hence the test now is not only of courage and energy, on the economic front as on the battlefield; it is also and even more a test of basic commitments, of sound value judgments implemented by swift, acute, logical intelligence.

Excessive impatience is a weakness, a danger. . . .

There have been moments of exasperation since the summer of 1940 when Nelson himself has felt that the President ought to yield to the demand that he appoint an economic boss whose orders to industry would have the full force of law—someone whose coercive powers would be virtually equivalent to those of the head of state and Commander in Chief in this emergency. But this feeling with him was transitory. Unlike many Big Businessmen brought into Government since the fall of France, he has come to understand and sympathize with the President's reluctance to permit any such concentration of authority in a single agency, a single administrator, as his critics often demand. The cause of this reluctance, he has become convinced, is not so much Roosevelt's appetite for personal power, great though this undoubtedly is, as it is his concern to preserve in practical operation the basic tenets of a free society.

This conclusion of Nelson's has derived in large part from his experience and observation of some key figures in the War Department and in the army's Services of Supply.

These men, in his view, display a ruthlessness of will and a narrow singleness of purpose which, were they invested with the coercive authority they obviously lust for, would irrevocably sacrifice the ends for which the war is being fought to the means of winning it on the battlefield. And the means they advocate are themselves of dubious efficacy, even in the military sense. It is far from certain that they would increase America's fighting efficiency: their net effect might be precisely the opposite—a lowering of national morale, a dissipation of economic energies. What *is* certain (so Nelson thinks) is that the country "saved" in this way would be fundamentally transformed; it would have become a kind of mirror-image, in essential respects, of the totalitarianism we loathe in our enemies.

Oversimplification—this is the great error of these men, Nelson thinks. They ask of every proposal a single simple question: Does it contribute *directly* to an increase of America's armed strength, serving the army's bureaucratic interests by giving it a wider margin for error and hence a greater freedom of choice? If it does, they favor the proposal; if it does not, they oppose it; and in either case their view has been decisive since, by the administrative arrangements prevailing until last evening, no civilian defense agency (certainly not Nelson's Priorities Board) has had the power to stand against them.

Nelson vividly remembers, he always will remember, a "lively little fracas" with the army and Under Secretary of War [Robert P.] Patterson over their insistence that two big aircraft manufacturing concerns, Lockheed and Douglas, be forced to cancel their contracts to provide between thirty and forty new commercial transports to major airlines. The army's argument was that this civilian "business as usual" interfered with the fulfillment of army contracts for war planes. Douglas and Lockheed vehemently denied that this was so, and were sustained by reports from production men sent out by the Priorities Board. The airlines placing the orders argued that the new planes were urgently needed to handle the increased traffic bound to result from the war emergency; they (the planes) should therefore be deemed an integral part of America's war strength, especially since they might be transferred to the army for troop transport if this should prove necessary. But Patterson and the army remained adamant. It was more *convenient* for the army to have the plane factories wholly at its disposal—and the convenience of the army took precedence in these men's minds over any civilian agency's wish or (even) necessity. So it appears to Nelson. It also appears to him that the arbitrary cancellation is motivated in part by a simple egoistic power-lust; the top echelon of army and War Department gains satisfaction from demonstrating to mere civilians in other agencies, and outside of Government, the fact that they have inferior status, they play subordinate roles, in the great drama of war.

Or consider the case of the first big contract-award for the manufacture of the sturdy, powerful, all-purpose, four-wheel-drive vehicle which has become known to the world as the *jeep*. This was back in the days of NDAC, when all army and navy contracts had to clear through [William S.] Knudsen's office (in his capacity as NDAC's Director of Production) before the final award could be made. Knudsen found that, of the three firms which had submitted bids for jeep making, namely, Ford, Bantam, and Willys, the latter's bid was lowest by some $560,000. Nevertheless, the army proposed to award the contract to Ford. Knudsen [former president of General Motors] refused to clear it. He insisted that the contract go to Willys, and stood firm in this decision against a delegation of high War Department officials who called upon him the next day. (He used his industry-gained prestige to overcome the delegation's vehement protests, saying: "If I know anything about production at all I know about producing motor cars. . . . This jeep is a motor car— and, gentlemen, I say Willys can make it.") The episode, in Nelson's view, is a case in point. It was more *convenient* for the army to deal with the giant Ford Motor Company than with relatively tiny Willys; the army had often worked before with Ford personnel, and there could be no doubt of Ford's ability to meet specifications. Of course this kind of operation throughout the war emergency would mean the use of taxpayers' money to extinguish small industry and promote monopoly. It might well lead toward a political economy closely similar to that envisaged in Mussolini's fascism. But such considerations seemed not to enter into the decision making of the army's top echelon.

Both episodes, Nelson thinks, are examples of oversimplification. They point up the dangerous error of selecting any single factor out of the enormous complex of variable factors in the present situation, assigning to it the status of an absolute, and then determining the value of every other factor altogether in terms of it. The only valid absolute is the *whole* of which the factors are integral parts and from which, as separate and distinct items, they are artificial abstractions. One must learn, therefore, to think "wholistically," determining the priorities of particular interests and acts by measuring them, ultimately, against the total need, the total action of the Republic as it fights for its survival as a democracy. One must learn to think in terms of balance and proportion within the whole, making often (necessarily) very close decisions as to which particular factor has or should have the greater weight when compared to another but doing it always in terms of the whole, the total process. If, for example, one is faced with the question of whether or not an aluminum-making plant should be expanded, he must answer it not only in terms of the need for more aluminum but also in terms of competing demands for structural steel, of which the supply is limited. The question becomes: Is the additional aluminum which the expanded plant will produce needed more than the steel that must be used in the plant's expansion? The answer can be arrived at only by considering both steel and aluminum as factors in the total Allied war effort.

Similar to such questions are *where* a defense plant should be located. Some months ago Nelson, as chairman of OPM's Plant Site Committee, reviewed an army proposal to purchase a twenty-thousand-acre block of the richest farmland in America in order to build upon it a big ordnance works. Judged solely in Army Engineering terms the selected site was ideal—but Nelson questioned whether its superiority in this respect over other possible sites on marginal or submarginal land was great enough to justify the removal from agricultural production of so much fertile soil. He raised the question with Ordnance, pointing out that a maximum production of food might well become of major importance to the total war effort. He indicated specifically other possible sites, only slightly less ideal than this one for Ordnance's special purpose, which had little or no value as farmland. Ordnance soon agreed with him; the plant site was shifted.

Labor versus management, Big versus Little Business, craft versus mass production—under these general headings rise innumerable specific issues, and each must be resolved, not as a simple halfway compromise between two opposing interests but, rather, in terms of the national purpose which both serve.

As regards labor versus management, Nelson will attempt to achieve solutions through the establishment of "labor-management" committees in war plants. These are not to be grievance committees, or collective bargaining committees; they are to be wholly devoted to ways and means of achieving a maximum efficiency of production. It must be noted in passing that labor, thus far, has been pressing harder than management for a full conversion of basic industries to war production. Everyone knows of the "Reuther Plan" for converting the auto industry (this industry is ultimately to account for some 20 per cent of the total war production) —a "plan" put forth by Walter P. Reuther, Director of General Motors' United Auto Workers of the CIO.

As regards Big versus Little Business, Nelson is forced to admit that Little Business has been getting and will continue to get "the dirty end of the stick." It suffers from the need to achieve speed and more speed in production. This need dictates the granting of giant contracts to industrial giants and the allocation to them of the materials needed to do the job, materials thereby denied the smaller firms having no war work to do. The latter, if they live at all, must generally live on subcontracts from the giants. On the other hand, insofar as the preservation of "The American Way" is the general objective of our war, Little Business must be granted the maximum possible protection—and Nelson with his colleagues must devote much attention to the problem of doing so through the granting of prime contracts to smaller firms whenever possible, through a proper distribution of subcontracts, and by stimulating small businessmen to "get in and fight" boldly and creatively for a share of the great work to be done. To this end, small businesses will increasingly pool their resources and augment their persuasive powers by working through local community "defense committees," designed to facilitate the obtaining of war contracts.

As regards craft versus mass production, the most precise calculations of relative benefits must be made in terms of the total effort, the ultimate objective. In general the decision will be in favor of mass production. When Packard, for instance, puts into mass production the Rolls-Royce motor used in British Spitfires—a motor built in England by highly expert hands—there may be some loss of perfection in individual motors, but this will be more than offset by having at hand unprecedented numbers of approximately perfect Rolls-Royce engines. The same kind of reasoning will lead Ford's [Charles E.] Sorensen to do all he can to freeze airplane designs once the Willow Run plant begins to turn out Consolidated bombers in huge numbers at great speed. He argues that the overwhelming numerical superiority we thus achieve in the shortest possible time more than offsets the advantages we might gain if we ripped production lines apart, interrupting output, every time a real or fancied design improvement appears on drafting boards. But of course this statistical approach to the matter does not appeal to individual combat pilots who may lose their lives because they encounter in battle enemy planes whose performance is superior to theirs. Nor is it possible wholly to ignore the improvements urged by battlefield experience, or by the design engineering of our enemies. At a certain point, quantitative superiority *is* offset by qualitative superiority, and the location of that precise point at which craftsmanship should prevail for the moment over mass production requires a very careful measurement of relative factors (the particular) against and within the whole (the general) of which they are elements.

Indeed, of all the questions Nelson will have now to deal with on the top policy level, only one, though of an importance overriding all the rest, seems to him answerable as a flat choice between opposing alternatives. This is the question of which is to have supreme control over the national economy as the war proceeds, the military or the civilian branches. The American democratic system, as established by the Constitution, requires all ultimate war-making powers to be vested firmly, unambiguously in civilian hands—and Nelson has found this principle, as applied to economics, to be accepted in practice as in theory by the officers of the chief army procurement agencies: the Quartermaster Corps, the Ordnance Department, the Corps of Engineers, the Signal Corps, the Medical Department. But on the top policy-making level of army and War Department, superior to these "working branches" of the army (he so designates them in invidious comparison with their superiors)—on this level he has encountered powerful men whom he suspects of a willingness if not a determination to break with American tradition and Constitution on this matter. His suspicion is destined to grow during the next two years into a conviction that these men (though they vehemently deny it) aim to impose military control upon the economy. Moreover they seem to him perfectly willing to use whatever means are at hand, fair or foul, to crush anyone who opposes them. Their manipulation of public opinion in order to further their aims or interests seems to him especially reprehensible; they have no compunction whatever about spreading through the channels of mass communication stories that are half true, or distorted in emphasis, or even (on crucial occasions) largely false. Already he is preparing to do battle against them, a battle whose tactics will be at first *sub rosa* and indirect but which (as we who look back may see) must lead ultimately into a head-on collision.

Part and parcel of Nelson's opposition to military control of the economy is his insistence that the widest possible latitude be maintained within which free choices and creative initiative can operate. The army, as a necessarily authoritarian organization, gives orders: its tendency is to tell a given industry not only *what* it is to make but also *how* the thing is to be made. Nelson is determined to avoid this. He is convinced that no man or group of men can possibly keep track of all the details, or distribute accurate emphases among all the interests, of the vast American economy. He therefore favors a kind of economic planning whereby definite goals are set and broad patterns of activity are applied but within which details and interests are left free, so far as may be, to call attention to themselves and even to take care of themselves.

And, indeed, as he breakfasts and then rides again through Rock Creek Park toward the Social Security Building, as he plunges into the details of his new assignment and is immersed in these through a long workday, a practical justification of his point of view is beginning to work itself out among airplane manufacturers on the West Coast. Last May the Congress had established a committee, headed by Senator Harry S Truman of Missouri, "to make a full and complete study and investigation of the operation of the program for the procurement and construction of supplies, materials, vehicles, aircraft, vessels, plants, camps and other articles and facilities in connection with the national defense." In the immediate aftermath of Pearl Harbor, when a deluge of orders poured in upon eight planemakers of Southern California, the Truman committee recommended that the President appoint a "czar" of the airplane industry. To prevent this, the heads of the companies "decided to offer the President an eight-president soviet to regiment our part of the industry," an organization that became known as the Aircraft War Production Council. Now cooperation has replaced competition among Lockheed, Douglas, Vultee, North American, Ryan, Consolidated, Vega, and Northrup. They have pooled their resources of material and talent and know-how, so that none of them has its production limited for lack of something another may have in good supply.

An important instance of this cooperation is about to be provided by Douglas and North American. The Douglas plant in El Segundo is manufacturing dive bombers for the navy, a rush order—and on a day that is in the near future as Nelson begins his work as WPB chairman, Douglas finds its tight production schedule threatened by a shortage of some two thousand feet of binding braid wire without which the planes cannot be bound into solid metallic units, thereby preventing dangerous buildups of static electricity during power dives. The crisis is acute, but the schedule is saved when the needed wire is found in a stockroom of North American. The dive bombers are then delivered in time for use in the mid- and far Pacific, where great and decisive naval actions impend. . . .

[In the summer of 1944, President Roosevelt journeyed to Pearl Harbor for a conference on Pacific war strategy with Admiral Chester Nimitz and General Douglas MacArthur. While he was away from Washington, a quarrel within the War Production Board, and between that board and the army, erupted into huge headlines.]

The quarrel was regarded by Donald Nelson, the WPB chairman, as the culmination of his long struggle to pre-

vent a totalitarian military domination of the civilian economy. It had to do with the reconversion of American industry from war to peace production, and it began when Nelson
on June 18 announced a four-point program:

(1) Revocation of WPB orders limiting the uses of aluminum
and magnesium, which had become very plentiful, so that manufacturers would be able to use these metals for the production of
essential civilian goods whenever manpower became available.

(2) Permission for any manufacturer to make and test a single
model of any product planned for postwar production.

(3) Provision for advance retooling by manufacturers, through
permission for the placing of unrated orders for tools and machinery needed for civilian production. . . . [An unrated order was
one that could not be filled until all those with priority ratings
had been filled.]

(4) A provision whereby a WPB regional director could au-
thorize a small manufacturer to go into production of civilian
goods, provided that the materials, the manufacturing capacity, or
the manpower involved was not needed for the war effort. ["Spot-
authorization," this was soon called.]

The program obviously meant "that there can be precious
little in the way of expanded civilian production in the immediate future," Nelson said. "But in the interest of war
production itself, and for the protection of the entire economy, it nevertheless is essential to prepare now for the return to civilian production. Just as industrial preparations
for war had to be started long before large-scale fighting began, so also the industrial preparations for peace must be
begun in plenty of time before the fighting ends."

The army and navy—though chiefly the army, through
Lieutenant General Brehon B. Somervell, Commanding
General of the Army Service Forces, and Robert P. Patterson, the Under Secretary of War—reacted violently against
this program. It was based on the dangerously dubious assumption that the war was about to end; it would promote
an exodus of labor from impermanent war jobs to permanent
peacetime civilian jobs, increasing the already excessive labor turnover in war plants; it would divert the attention and
energies of management from the present needs of military

production to the future possibilities of civilian production; and it would deny to the army that flexibility as to kind and amount of matériel made necessary by the fluctuating fortunes of war. Its overall effect could be disastrous on the fighting fronts in the months ahead. So ran the army argument. Nelson flatly denied every part of it and, indeed, doubted that it frankly expressed the real convictions of those who advanced it. He suspected hidden motives. So did Senator Truman in his capacity as chairman of the Truman committee. In a special statement released to the press on July 8, Truman described the announced Nelson program as an effort to bring about "an orderly resumption of civilian production in areas where there is no manpower shortage and with materials that are not required for war production." The program, he went on to say,

has been opposed by some selfish business groups that want to see their competitors kept idle until they finish their war contracts. It has also been opposed by army and navy representatives who want to create a surplus of manpower with the hope that the consequent pressure on unemployed workers would result in some of them shifting to occupations or areas in which there is still a manpower shortage.

The latter point was the crux of the openly stated matter, in Nelson's view. There had been increasingly frequent cutbacks in military orders during recent months. These had created localized unemployment, some of it severe. In other areas, and in certain kinds of jobs, there were acute manpower shortages. But to assume as the army assumed that a deliberate creation of "pools of unemployment" in towns A and B and C would, through forced migration, relieve manpower shortages in towns D and E and F, hundreds of miles away—to assume this was to betray a woeful ignorance of the nature of the labor supply, of American production techniques, and of human psychology in general.

Workers are not all cut to a pattern as were the men of Frederick the Great's Prussian Guards [said Donald Nelson]. They follow many skills and trades, most of which are not learned instantaneously. It does no good at all to cry that you need five hundred workers; the question is, What kinds of workers? If you need welders, the existence of many thousands of unemployed linotype operators will do you no good whatever.

The army argued that there should be no revival of the civilian economy anywhere so long as there was labor shortage in a single war plant, which meant (in Nelson's words) that "you couldn't employ idle die-setters in Cleveland if a factory in Phoenix needed welders."

So obviously fatuous was this openly stated argument that Nelson could not but believe it designed, at least in part, for the achievement of unstated aims. Perhaps its ulterior motive lay among those "selfish business groups" (Big Business) to which Senator Truman had referred and with which officers of the Army Supply Services had close, friendly ties. Certainly there were some in Big Business who argued strongly if privately that the war must not be permitted to "change the pattern" of American industry and that to prevent this the Government should not permit or encourage individual reconversions by relaxing its economic controls but should instead use these controls to insure the restoration, so far as possible, of the *status quo ante bellum* [prewar situation]. There should be a precisely defined reconversion period, according to this view. During it each producer would be permitted to manufacture only such kinds of things as he had made before the war, and in numbers that were in direct ratio to his production figures during a stated prewar base period. Thus all manufacturers of a given product would resume its manufacture simultaneously, would not be permitted to shift to new products until the defined reconversion period had ended, and would face no new competition during this period. Small wonder that the proposal was not loudly pressed in public by its most ardent supporters! Its easily discernible effect would be the end of such industrial democracy as yet remained in America. The proposed reconversion period must be, at least at the outset, one of rising unemployment and decreasing supplies of consumer goods— a period of depression during which the incomes of common

folk were drastically reduced while the prices of the things
they must buy were upheld by Government controls and imposed market scarcities. And at its end there would be few
if any small manufacturers left in the country. Monopoly
industry would reign supreme over the economy; linked to
the army in a giant industrial-military complex, it might
well rule a totalitarian United States.

Indeed, the whole army approach to manpower and reconversion problems was, in Nelson's view, but another expression of the authoritarian, totalitarian mind against
which he had had to struggle for two long years. Such a mind
had a penchant for single prescriptions and blanket solutions. It lacked the precision or was too lazy to make the dis-
criminatory judgments upon which the preservation of individual liberty, or of any kind of recognized individualism,
depends. And it was driven by a lust for personal power un-
mitigated by concern for the rights and sufferings of other
individual men and women. In actual reality, excessive labor
turnover in war plants was a multiple ill for which there
could be no single prescription, a multiple problem that
could not be adequately covered by any blanket solution. In
one plant the problem could be solved simply by lighting
a previously unlighted parking area. In another it could be
solved by staggering the open hours of grocery stores and
other facilities so that night-shift workers could make use of
them. In a third, it could be solved by removal of an incom-
petent or disagreeable plant manager. Each case was different; each required its own unique handling within a general
framework of policy. Those who would shape true solutions
must apply to each problem, not the romantic's forceful will
but the realist's critical intelligence. . . .

[Soon the] WPB was itself split into warring factions by
the quarrel with the army. Charles E. Wilson [on leave as
president of General Electric], Nelson's principal subordinate . . . , was inclined to agree with the army, at least to the
extent that he felt the announced reconversion plan might
be premature. Other WPB vice chairmen agreed with the

army not only as regards the *when* but also as regards the
how of reconversion, the army's *how* being that of a precisely
defined and rigorously controlled reconversion period. Wilson and these others soon found themselves attacked in public as enemies of free enterprise and promoters of monopoly
who, it was clearly implied, stood to make private profit from
the public policy they favored. Moreover, and worse, they
believed (were led by the army to believe) that the attacks
upon them had their secret source in Nelson's own office—an
allegation Nelson vehemently denied. Meanwhile, Nelson
himself was under public attack as the army released sly stories of an alleged "production crisis" in contexts indicating
that WPB was responsible for it. (In point of fact, according to Nelson, there was no "production crisis," and such
material shortages as existed were generally due to the army's
own mistakes in making premature cutbacks and then,
months later, restoring them.)

THE ORDEAL OF DONALD NELSON—CONTINUED [6]

At this critical juncture, [summer 1944] Nelson became
ill and was hospitalized. Wilson was left in charge of WPB.
Predictably, nothing happened. Senator Harry S Truman
demanded that Wilson issue Nelson's projected reconversion
orders. ... But even so distinguished a Senator as Truman ...
could not budge the immovable and implacable military-industrial complex, then in its infancy but already a titan.
Calls for action only led to a Military propaganda campaign
that, in many instances, flew in the clear face of truth.

General Somervell fired the opening salvo on July 14,
1944. He declared the loss of manpower in war plants had
created a shortage of larger shells, so that "smaller shells and
even rifle and machine gun fire" had to be substituted,

[6] From *The Warfare State*, by Fred J. Cook. Macmillan. '62. p 62-3. Reprinted with permission of The Macmillan Company from *The Warfare State*
by Fred J. Cook. © by Fred J. Cook, 1962. Mr. Cook is an author and journalist,
three times winner of the New York Newspaper Guild's Page One Award while
a reporter for the New York *World-Telegram*.

"which inevitably meant closer fighting and greater loss of American lives." This statement touched off a wave of charges designed to show that GIs were dying needlessly in the cause of reconversion. Ship construction, it was alleged, was being delayed by workers "quitting to take peacetime jobs." Somervell insisted the situation was so serious changes had had to be made in battle plans. The War Department solemnly declared that "a lag in tire production . . . was endangering the prospects of early victory."

Yet the WPB Progress Report for July, the most accurate barometer of what was actually being produced compared with what was actually needed, concluded flatly that "supplies range from a low of eleven months for the noncombat vehicles to *twenty-two months for the ammunition programs. . . .*" (Italics added.) There was enough small arms ammunition, the report said, to last five years. Significantly, this document with its unwelcome figures didn't see the light of day at the time. The Military demanded and secured its suppression.

All this time, while the Military was carrying the ball out front, Wilson and his Big Business associates were being industrious little beavers behind the scenes. One graphic example of their handiwork may be seen in the neat alteration obtained in the plan to permit manufacture of refrigerators. The order as originally drafted called for the manufacture of "Domestic Mechanical Refrigerators—Except Electric." A few days later, this wording was changed to: "Domestic Mechanical Refrigerators—Except Electric *and Gas.*" (Italics added.) The addition of those last two words made it certain that Servel, which had been anticipating war cutbacks and idle facilities, would not be able to jump into the domestic refrigerator market ahead of GE.

Such a long-continuing power struggle, fought both overtly in the columns of the press and covertly in the back alleys of bureaucracy, could not continue indefinitely. With a presidential election campaign coming up in the fall of

1944, [Franklin D.] Roosevelt decided to put a lid on the disturbing tempest. He sent Nelson off on a mission to China. The intention apparently was to elevate Wilson to the WPB chairmanship in Nelson's absence, but leaked stories in the press kicked up such a storm that Roosevelt drew back from making the appointment. Wilson, in disgust, resigned and returned to his beloved GE, and Julius Krug was appointed acting WPB chairman under strict orders from Roosevelt to avoid controversy. This restriction practically insured that very little that needed doing would ever get done.

The aftermath of this bitter quarrel shed much revealing light on the character of the Military-Big Business campaign that had strangled reconversion in the name of patriotism. So much steel was produced in 1944 that the armed services couldn't possibly consume it all and had to turn back 300,000 tons of their fourth-quarter quota. Even the Military, who had promoted scare headlines about war shortages, had to admit there had been little truth to its claims. General Somervell, appearing before the Senate defense investigating committee, acknowledged that "no one has so far suffered from a lack of supplies." Testifying to the very opposite of what he had publicly proclaimed, he conceded that shortages had not interfered with the conduct of the war. Significantly, he admitted that army propaganda about ammunition shortages, dramatized on radio by conversations ostensibly recorded between soldiers in battle, was deceptive. The Senate committee concluded that "insufficient production . . . has not been the cause of the shortage of weapons and ammunition at the front."

Such is the history of the reconversion battle. What it says is clear. The combination of the Military and Big Business had ignored facts, had employed callous propaganda, had defied senators and congressmen, had brought about the downfall of Donald Nelson, and had succeeded in stalling reconversion until giant corporations, bloated to several times their former size by Government-subsidized wartime plant expansions, could get back into the civilian market and protect their hold on the civilian economy. This was a process that clearly was the antithesis of democracy. The economic oligarchies had been protected at the expense of small business, at the expense of labor, at the expense of the consumer—in other words, at the expense of about nine tenths of the nation.

ARMS AND INDUSTRY AFTER WORLD WAR II [7]

A Bureau of the Budget document published in 1946, *The United States at War*, says that the army tried to gain "total control of the nation, its manpower, its facilities, its economy," and when [President Franklin D.] Roosevelt or [Donald] Nelson [head of the War Production Board] blocked this scheme temporarily, "the military leaders took another approach to secure the same result. . . ." Since war expenditures accounted for more than one out of every three dollars of gross national product in 1945 the War Department felt it had a legitimate right to run the economy.

This view was reinforced by business leaders in and out of Government—e.g. James Forrestal of Dillon, Read and Charles E. Wilson of General Electric. What the nation needed, said Wilson in January 1944, was "a permanent war economy." He proposed that every large company choose a liaison man with the armed forces (to be commissioned as a colonel in the reserve), because military preparedness "must be, once and for all, a continuing program and not the creature of an emergency." Under his scheme Congress would be "limited to voting the needed funds" while the Military and Big Business would run the show.

Why did we need a "permanent" war economy? For the record, the American people were told in lurid redundancy that both we and our allies were in danger of a military at-

[7] From *The Military-Industrial Complex*, by Sidney Lens, author, editor, labor union director. Philadelphia. Pilgrim Press. '70. p 18-23, 32. Copyright © 1970 by Sidney Lens. Used by permission.

tack from Soviet Russia. "The Pentagon line," said Colonel
William H. Neblett, national president of the Reserve Officers Association, "was that we were living in a state of undeclared emergency; that war with Russia was just around
the corner. . . ."

Long before the Soviets had acquired their first atom
bomb or even tested one, Lieutenant General Leslie R.
Groves warned that in the first five hours of an atomic attack
40 million Americans would be killed, and General Carl A.
Spaatz explained that it would be too late for defense after
the atomic bombs started falling. By drawing this ominous
picture the military was able to win approval of a $12 billion
budget for fiscal 1948.

But a whole host of scholars—D. F. Fleming, William
Appleman Williams, Gabriel Kolko, David Horowitz, Richard Barnet, Marcus Raskin, to name a few—now question the
assumption that the Soviet Union was preparing for a military invasion either of Western Europe or the United States.
The Russian dictator, Joseph Stalin, was brutal in dealing
with his own people, but it is often forgotten that for a few
years after the war, he assumed an exceedingly moderate
posture elsewhere. His nation had lost 25 million people in
the war, was desperately in need of aid for rebuilding, and
continued for a long time to nurture hopes of coexistence.
Far from being revolutionary, Stalin in those years put the
damper on revolution wherever he could.

The Soviet leader, reports historian Fleming, "scoffed at
communism in Germany, urged the Italian Reds to make
peace with the monarchy, did his best to induce Mao Tse-
tung to come to terms with the Kuomintang and angrily demanded of Tito that he back the monarchy, thus fulfilling
his (Stalin's) bargain with Chuchill. . . ."

Communists in this period joined "bourgeois governments" throughout Europe and worked hard to rebuild tat-
tered economies. "The key" to reconstruction in France,
wrote Joseph Alsop in July 1946, was "the enthusiastic col-

laboration of the French Communist party. The Communists control the most important unions of the CGT [Confédération Générale du Travail] the great French confederation of labor unions. Communist leadership has been responsible for such surprising steps as acceptance by the key French unions of a kind of modified piecework system. . . . Reconstruction comes first, is the party line." The Communists dissuaded their followers in North Africa from taking the path of revolution, thus leaving the field to non-Communist nationalists like Ahmed Ben Bella. Stalin ordered Soviet troops out of Azerbaijan—northwest Iran—thereby liquidating the Communist regime under Jafar Pishevari. He failed to lift a finger while British forces put down an EAM [the National Liberation Front] revolt in Greece, a circumstance for which he won lavish praise from no less a personage than Winston Churchill. Stalin, wrote Churchill, "adhered strictly and faithfully to our agreement of October, and during all the long weeks of fighting the Communists in the streets of Athens not one word of reproach came from *Pravda* or *Izvestia*." As for China—according to the British Royal Institute of International Affairs—Stalin tried to dissuade Mao, as late as 1948, from an "all-out offensive to crush the Kuomintang and seize power."

Stalin *did* torpedo democratic elections in Poland and *did* help satellite parties, with small popular followings, to gain the helm in Eastern Europe. In the passions of Cold War, however, the American memory is letter perfect on the "broken pledges" of Moscow, but tends toward amnesia on the broken pledges of the West. We forget that in addition to Yalta, one of the fundamental documents of World War II was the Atlantic Charter signed by Franklin Roosevelt and Churchill "somewhere in the Atlantic" four months before Pearl Harbor. Point Two of the Charter bound the Western Alliance to "no territorial changes that do not accord with the freely expressed wishes of the peoples concerned." Point Three—most important of the eight statements of purpose—

promised "sovereign rights and self-government restored to those who have been forcibly deprived of them." These points were violated repeatedly by the West as it tried to suppress nationalist revolutions in Madagascar (1943-44), Greece (1944), Algeria, Tunisia, Morocco (1945), Indochina and Indonesia (1945-46) all of them *before* the Soviets had begun to renege on pledges of elections in Poland, and after it had become obvious that a *modus vivendi* with the West was unlikely.

Whatever the rights and wrongs of the Cold War, however, many prominent Americans recognized that the "Communist threat" of the 1940s was not one of military invasion but of encouraging nationalist revolutions—if and when Stalin decided to do so. John Foster Dulles [who became Secretary of State in the Eisenhower Administration], . . . conceded in March 1949 that the Soviet government "does not contemplate the use of war as an instrument of its national policy. I do not know any responsible official, military or civilian, in this Government or any government, who believes that the Soviet government now plans conquest by open military aggression."

David Horowitz has assembled a half dozen similar statements by leading figures. James Forrestal recorded in his diary June 10, 1946, that he thought the Russians "would not move this summer—in fact, at any time." General Walter Bedell Smith on August 3, 1948, two months after the Berlin blockade, advised the War Council "that the Russians do not want war." His successor, Admiral Alan G. Kirk, was reported by *U.S. News & World Report* six months after the onset of the Korean War, as seeing "no signs in Moscow that Russia expects war now. . . . Currently Admiral Kirk detects none of the telltale signs of war that the experts watch for." Reminiscing on the early Cold War period in May 1965, George Kennan [former U.S. Ambassador] reinforced the Dulles estimate: "It was perfectly clear to anyone with even a rudimentary knowledge of the Russia of that day that the

Soviet leaders had no intention of attempting to advance their cause by launching military attacks with their own armed forces across frontiers."

General Douglas MacArthur—no dove—said in mid-1957: "Our Government has kept us in a perpetual state of fear— kept us in a continuous stampede of patriotic fervor—with the cry of a grave national emergency. . . . Yet, in retrospect, these disasters seem never to have happened, seem never to have been real." Even President Nixon raised a few eyebrows early in his Administration by referring to the Soviet Union's military stance as "defensive," rather than offensive.

The United States, it seems clear, backed itself into the military-industrial stall not out of fear of Soviet invasion, but out of other motives. This does not mean that the misgivings of American citizens over purges and authoritarianism in the Soviet orbit was disingenuous or synthetic. It wasn't; many alarming things were taking place in Stalin's domain. But the men at the levers of power in America interpreted the word *defense* quite differently from its traditional meaning. Historian William Appleman Williams quotes congressmen at the end of the war who felt that the nation's purpose must be to seek "world power as a trustee for civilization." Henry B. Luce, publisher of *Time*, called this the "American century," and business spokesmen referred to the American role as "missionaries of capitalism and democracy," presumably equating the two.

Most forthright of all perhaps was Under Secretary of State Dean Acheson, who told a congressional committee in 1944 that "it is a problem of markets. . . . We have got to see that what the country produces is used and is sold under financial arrangements which make its production possible." Under a different system, he admitted, "you could use the entire production of the country in the United States," but under our present form of free enterprise, the Government "must look to foreign markets." If it didn't "it seems clear that we are in for a very bad time . . . having the most far-

reaching consequences upon our economic and social system." America's goal in the postwar world, it seems, was not
quite as eleemosynary as its public proclamations pretended;
a dollar sign lurked in the shadows.

Shortly after Harry Truman became President, he told a
visitor, according to Williams, "that the Russians would
soon be put in their places; and that the United States would
then take the lead in running the world in a way that the
world ought to be run." In a March 1947 speech at Baylor
University that has never received the attention it deserved,
Truman argued that freedom was more urgent than peace,
and that in the final analysis it could be assured only through
the worldwide prevalence of "free enterprise." Freedom—
of enterprise, speech, worship, assembly, all interdependent
on each other—could not exist where the Government does
the planning and operates foreign trade. The enemy of free
enterprise was "regimented economies," and "unless we act,
and act decisively," said Truman, those regimented economies would become "the pattern of the next century." To
guard against the danger he urged that "the whole world
should adopt the American system." That system "could
survive in America only *if it became a world system*." (Italics
added.)

Here in defensive rhetoric Truman was explaining what
it was about communism that threatened us—making it necessary to "act decisively." Certainly its military machine
posed a challenge, though as Dulles, [James V.] Forrestal
[wartime Secretary of the Navy and the first Secretary
of Defense], and others clearly understood, it was not a decisive one. What concerned Truman and the military men
who ran his State Department, was the issue of "free" versus
"regimented" economies. The Soviet orbit's own economy
was "regimented," and if the new nations—whose revolutions were supported by the Soviets—were to become similarly "regimented," American free enterprise would find a large
area of the world closed off to its trade and investment, as

well as its needs in raw materials. Early in the century the
United States had been relatively self-sufficient and had a
small . . . [surplus] of raw materials for export; but by mid-
century it was using 35 to 40 per cent of the free world's supply of basic commodities for which it paid $5 to $6 billion
a year. To guarantee markets and supplies a new strategy
was needed therefore—economic, political, and military—to
make the American system a world system.

The military-industrial complex advanced inexorably to
further this purpose—what Professor Neal D. Houghton calls
"global imperialism," by contrast with the "continental imperialism" the United States practiced in the nineteenth
century when it expanded westward, and the episodic imperialism, say in Latin America, of the early part of this century. The traditional form of imperialism—the naked occupation of foreign lands—was no longer feasible or desirable
at the end of World War II. But other means were at hand,
and it was these that the military-industrial complex put
into magnificent practice to defend and extend the free enterprise system against the regimented ones. . . .

The military-industrial complex, it is clear, was born
out of motives more earthy than its sponsors imply. If its
function is to "preserve the peace," its definition of the
word *peace* is synonymous with global expansion.

SECURITY AS DEFINED BY THE
MILITARY ESTABLISHMENT [8]

What General [David M.] Shoup [Commandant of the
U.S. Marine Corps in the early 1960s, now retired], calls the
"new militarism" is an outgrowth of the Second World War.
The Federal Government came to play a major managerial
role in the economy and to help create and to dispose of a
significant share of the national wealth. Within the Federal

[8] From *The Economy of Death*, by Richard J. Barnet, codirector of The
Institute for Policy Studies in Washington, D.C. Atheneum. '69. p 68-73.
Adapted from *The Economy of Death* by Richard J. Barnet. Copyright © 1969
by Richard J. Barnet. Reprinted by permission of Atheneum Publishers.

bureaucracy the balance of power shifted decisively to those agencies which handled military power. In 1939 the Federal Government had about 800,000 civilian employees, about 10 per cent of whom worked for national-security agencies. At the end of the war the figure approached 4 million, of whom more than 75 per cent were in military-related activities.

Not only did the war radically shift the balance of power in the Federal bureaucracy, catapulting the Military Establishment from a marginal institution without a constituency to a position of command over the resources of a whole society; it also redefined the traditional tasks of the military. The traditional semantic barriers between "political" and "military" functions were eroded; in the development and execution of strategy, the military were deep in politics. The major decisions of the war, those with the greatest obvious political impact, were made by the President, the Joint Chiefs of Staff, and Harry Hopkins [special assistant to President Franklin D. Roosevelt]. The Joint Chiefs prepared for diplomatic conferences, negotiated with the Allies. In the war theatres the military commanders, Eisenhower and MacArthur, were supreme. Each obtained the power to pass on all civilians sent to his theatre and to censor their dispatches. "Through these controls of overseas communications," the military commentator Walter Millis observed, "JCS was in a position to be informed, forewarned, and therefore forearmed, to a degree no civilian agency could match."

At a time when Stalingrad was still under siege and it would have taken a lively imagination to conjure up a Soviet threat of world domination, United States military planners had already begun planning a huge postwar military machine. As the war ended, the army demanded a ground force capable of expanding to 4.5 million men within a year. The navy thought it wanted to keep 600,000 men, 371 major combat ships, 5000 auxiliaries, and a "little air force" of 8000 planes. The air force also had specific plans. It wanted to be a separate service and to have a seventy-group force with 400,000 men. With these plans the top military officers made it clear that they were through being fire-fighters called in when the diplomats had failed.

Under the pressure of war, new military instruments for manipulating the politics of other countries had been developed. Those who had put them together argued that the United States would need them in the postwar world, whatever the political environment. Thus the Joint Chiefs of Staff argued successfully for retaining most of the network of bases acquired in the war. The thinking of General William Donovan, the creator of OSS, America's first spy agency, shows the indestructibility of bureaucracies. His assistant Robert H. Alcorn has described his views:

> With the vision that had characterized his development of . . . [Office of Strategic Services], General Donovan had, before leaving the organization, made provision for the future of espionage in our country's way of life. Through both Government and private means he had indicated the need for a long-range, built-in espionage network. He saw the postwar years as periods of confusion and readjustment affording the perfect opportunity to establish such networks. We were everywhere already, he argued, and it was only wisdom and good policy to dig in, quietly and efficiently, for the long pull. Overseas branches of large corporations, the expanding business picture, the rebuilding of war areas, Government programs for economic, social and health aid to foreign lands, all these were made to order for the infiltration of espionage agents.

A nation that for almost four years had performed stunning managerial feats in moving armies across seas, in producing clouds of airplanes, in training destructive power on an enemy with marvelous efficiency, and, finally, in extracting the abject surrender of two of the leading industrial nations of the world without having enemy soldiers or bombs on its soil or its wealth impaired, was ready to put its confidence in force as the primary instrument of politics. Americans, who had often felt swindled in the dreary game of diplomacy, looked in awe at the immense changes they had wrought in the world with their military power.

To maintain and extend their power in the postwar period, the military have been able to draw on a varied and effective arsenal. The most important weapon has been organization. As we have seen, the military bureaucracies came out of the war with their structures intact. Despite the rapid demobilization of millions of men and the sharp reduction of the defense budget from more than $80 billion to $11.7 billion in the first three postwar years, the institutional relationships of the Economy of Death created in the war were preserved and expanded. In this process the Military Establishment exploited two other weapons to the fullest: secrecy and fear.

In a bureaucracy knowledge is power. The Military Establishment has made particularly effective use of its jealously guarded monopoly of information on national-security matters. It has defined the threats, chosen the means to counteract them, and evaluated its own performance. Critics have been disarmed by the classification system and the standard official defense of policy, "If you only knew what I know." Academic consultants who have made their living advising the Department of Defense and writing about national-security affairs have protected their security clearances by discreetly accepting the Pentagon's assumptions. Except for a handful of Quakers, radicals, independent scientists, and incorrigible skeptics, no one during the 1940s and 1950s challenged the growing power of the Military. The fact that the Pentagon was assuming a central position in American life was obvious. But the justification seemed equally obvious, and the danger was ignored.

Because of its exclusive hold on top-secret truth, the Pentagon was in a position to scare the public into supporting whatever programs the Administration put forward. The Department of Defense became a Ministry of Fear issuing regular warnings about a highly exaggerated threat of a Soviet attack in Europe and a nuclear strike against the United

States long before the Soviets had the means to carry it out. Joseph R. McCarthy was a helpful ally in creating a climate of fear until he turned against the army in a last suicidal gesture. But McCarthyism preceded McCarthy. Alger Hiss, the old China hands, the Poland losers, the Czechoslovakia losers, and other "vendors of compromise" in the State Department, as Senator John F. Kennedy would later call them, became tabloid celebrities long before Senator McCarthy advertised his "list" of 205 known Communists in the State Department. In this atmosphere anyone who dared to suggest that the country was spending too much money on defense was obviously either a traitor with a plan to leave the country "naked to attack" or a coward who preferred to be red rather than dead.

Military officers constantly held up to the public the specters of Hitler and Pearl Harbor. The only security in a dangerous and irrational world was to run it. On his office wall the first Secretary of Defense, James Forrestal, hung a framed card on which was printed the official lesson of World War II: "We will never have peace until the strongest army and the strongest navy are in the hands of the world's most powerful nation." It was now America's turn to be Number One in the world and to play out the historical role of earlier empires. It did not matter that the age of empire was over or that the age of nuclear weapons had come. In military bureaucracies it is standard procedure to pursue the most promising strategy for preventing the last war.

THE EISENHOWER MEMORANDUM: SCIENTIFIC AND TECHNOLOGICAL RESOURCES AS MILITARY ASSETS [9]

[In the spring of 1946, when he was Chief of Staff of the United States Army, General Dwight D. Eisenhower prepared the following memorandum. It is a crucially impor-

[9] Text from *Pentagon Capitalism: The Political Economy of War*, by Seymour Melman, professor of industrial engineering, Columbia University. McGraw. '70. Appendix A p 231-4.

tant statement of national policy insofar as it provided the guidelines along which the close cooperation between the army, industry, the universities, and organizations of scientists and technologists, developed during World War II, was tightened and solidified into a machine-like "complex" during the decades that followed. The memorandum was found by Professor Gabriel Kolko among the Henry L. Stimson papers in the Sterling Library of Yale University; it was first published as an appendix to Seymour Melman's *Pentagon Capitalism: The Political Economy of War* (McGraw-Hill Book Company, 1970).—Ed.]

Memorandum for Directors and Chiefs of War Department General and Special Staff Divisions and Bureaus and the Commanding Generals of the Major Commands:

Subject: *Scientific and Technological Resources as Military Assets*

The recent conflict has demonstrated more convincingly than ever before the strength our nation can best derive from the integration of all of our national resources in time of war. It is of the utmost importance that the lessons of this experience be not forgotten in the peacetime planning and training of the army. The future security of the nation demands that all those civilian resources which by conversion or redirection constitute our main support in time of emergency be associated closely with the activities of the army in time of peace.

The lessons of the last war are clear. The military effort required for victory threw upon the army an unprecedented range of responsibilities, many of which were effectively discharged only through the invaluable assistance supplied by our cumulative resources in the natural and social sciences and the talents and experience furnished by management and labor. The armed forces could not have won the war alone. Scientists and businessmen contributed techniques and weapons which enabled us to outwit and overwhelm the enemy. Their understanding of the army's needs made possible the highest degree of cooperation. This pattern of integration must be translated into a peacetime counterpart which will not merely familiarize the army with the progress made in science and industry, but draw into our planning for national security all the civilian resources which can contribute to the defense of the country.

Success in this enterprise depends to a large degree on the cooperation which the nation as a whole is willing to contribute. However, the army as one of the main agencies responsible for the defense of the nation has the duty to take the initiative in promoting closer relation between civilian and military interests. It must establish definite policies and administrative leadership which will make possible even greater contributions from science, technology, and management than during the last war.

In order to ensure the full use of our national resources in case of emergency, the following general policies will be put into effect:

(1) *The army must have civilian assistance in military planning as well as for the production of weapons.* Effective long-range military planning can be done only in the light of predicted developments in science and technology. As further scientific achievements accelerate the tempo and expand the area of our operations, this interrelationship will become of even greater importance. In the past we have often deprived ourselves of vital help by limiting our use of scientific and technological resources to contracts for equipment. More often than not we can find much of the talent we need for comprehensive planning in industry or universities. Proper employment of this talent requires that the civilian agency shall have the benefit of our estimates of future military problems and shall work closely with plans and the research and development authorities. A most effective procedure is the letting of contracts for aid in planning. The use of such a procedure will greatly enhance the validity of our planning as well as ensure sounder strategic equipment programs.

74   The Reference Shelf

(2) *Scientists and industrialists must be given the greatest possible freedom to carry out their research.* The fullest utilization by the army of the civilian resources of the nation cannot be procured merely by prescribing the military characteristics and requirements of certain types of equipment. Scientists and industrialists are more likely to make new and unsuspected contributions to the development of the army if detailed directions are held to a minimum. The solicitation of assistance under these conditions would not only make available to the army talents and experience otherwise beyond our reach, but also establish mutual confidence between ourselves and civilians. It would familiarize them with our fundamental problems and strengthen greatly the foundation upon which our national security depends.

(3) *The possibility of utilizing some of our industrial and technological resources as organic parts of our military structure in time of emergency should be carefully examined.* The degree of cooperation with science and industry achieved during the recent war should by no means be considered the ultimate. There appears little reason for duplicating within the army an outside organization which by its experience is better qualified than we are to carry out some of our tasks. The advantages to our nation in economy and to the army in efficiency are compelling reasons for this procedure.

(4) *Within the army we must separate responsibility for research and development from the functions of procurement, purchase, storage and distribution.* Our experience during the war and the experience of industry in time of peace indicate the need for such a policy. The inevitable gap between the scientist or technologist and the user can be bridged, as during the last war, by field experimentation with equipment still in the developmental stage. For example, restricted-visibility operations with the aid of radar, such as blind bombing and control of tactical air, were made

possible largely by bringing together technologists who knew the potentialities of the equipment and field commanders familiar with combat conditions and needs. Future cooperation of this type requires that research and development groups have authority to procure experimental items for similar tests.

(5) *Officers of all arms and services must become fully aware of the advantages which the army can derive from the close integration of civilian talent with military plans and developments.* This end cannot be achieved merely by sending officers to universities for professional training. It is true that the army's need for officers well trained in the natural and social sciences requires a thorough program of advanced study for selected military personnel, but in addition we must supply inducements which will encourage these men in the continued practical application of scientific and technological thought to military problems. A premium must be placed on professional attainments in the natural and social sciences as well as other branches of military science. Officers in each arm and service must familiarize themselves as much as possible with progress and plans made in other branches. Only then can the army obtain the administrative and operative talents essential to its task and mutual understanding by the arms and services of their respective problems.

In general, the more we can achieve the objectives indicated above with respect to the cultivation, support and direct use of outside resources, the more energy will we have left to devote to strictly military problems for which there are no outside facilities or which for special security reasons can only be handled by the military. In fact, it is our responsibility deliberately to examine all outside resources as to adequacy, diversity, and geographical distribution and to ensure their full utilization as factors of security. It is our job to take the initiative to promote the development of new resources, if our national security indicates the need. It is our duty to support broad research programs in educational institutions, in industry, and in whatever field might be of importance to the army. Close integration of military and civilian resources will not only directly benefit the army, but indirectly contribute to the nation's security, as civilians are prepared for their role in an emergency by the experience gained in time of peace. The association of military and civilians in educational institutions and industry will level barriers, engender mutual understanding, and lead to the cultivation of friendships invaluable for future cooperation. The realization of our objectives places upon us, the military, the challenge to make our professional officers the equals in knowledge and training of civilians in similar fields and make our professional environment as inviting as those outside.

In the interest of cultivating to the utmost the integration of civilian and military resources and of securing the most effective unified direction of our research and development activities, this responsibility is being consolidated in a separate section on the highest War Department level. The director of this section will be directly supported by one or more civilians, thus ensuring full confidence of both the military and the civilian in this undertaking. By the rotation of civilian specialists in this capacity we should have the benefit of broad guidance and should be able to furnish science and industry with a firsthand understanding of our problems and objectives. By developing the general policies outlined above under the leadership of the Director of Research and Development the army will demonstrate the value it places upon science and technology and further the integration of civilian and military resources.

Signed by General Eisenhower
on April 27, 1946.

A PRESIDENTIAL WARNING [10]

[What General Eisenhower had proposed in his memorandum of April 27, 1946, had become an awesome reality by January 17, 1961, when President Eisenhower, after eight years in the White House, made his famous Farewell to the Nation address. Following are parts III and IV of that address.—Ed.]

III

Throughout America's adventure in free government our basic purposes have been to keep the peace, to foster progress in human achievement, and to enhance liberty, dignity, and integrity among people and among nations. To strive for less would be unworthy of a free and religious people. Any failure traceable to arrogance or our lack of comprehension or readiness to sacrifice would inflict upon us grievous hurt both at home and abroad.

Progress toward these noble goals is persistently threatened by the conflict now engulfing the world. It commands our whole attention, absorbs our very beings. We face a hostile ideology—global in scope, atheistic in character, ruthless in purpose, and insidious in method. Unhappily the danger it poses promises to be of indefinite duration. To meet it successfully there is called for not so much the emotional and transitory sacrifices of crisis but rather those which enable us to carry forward steadily, surely, and without complaint the burdens of a prolonged and complex struggle— with liberty the stake. Only thus shall we remain, despite every provocation, on our charted course toward permanent peace and human betterment.

Crises there will continue to be. In meeting them, whether foreign or domestic, great or small, there is a recurring temptation to feel that some spectacular and costly action could become the miraculous solution to all current difficul-

[10] Parts III-IV of "Farewell Radio and Television Address to the American People, January 17, 1961," by President Dwight D. Eisenhower. Text from *Department of State Bulletin.* 44:180-1. F. 6, '61.

ties. A huge increase in newer elements of our defense, development of unrealistic programs to cure every ill in agriculture, a dramatic expansion in basic and applied research —these and many other possibilities, each possibly promising in itself, may be suggested as the only way to the road we wish to travel.

But each proposal must be weighed in the light of a broader consideration: the need to maintain balance in and among national programs—balance between the private and the public economy, balance between cost and hoped-for advantage, balance between the clearly necessary and the comfortably desirable, balance between our essential requirements as a nation and the duties imposed by the nation upon the individual, balance between actions of the moment and the national welfare of the future. Good judgment seeks balance and progress; lack of it eventually finds imbalance and frustration.

The record of many decades stands as proof that our people and their Government have, in the main, understood these truths and have responded to them well in the face of stress and threat. But threats, new in kind or degree, constantly arise. I mention two only.

IV

A vital element in keeping the peace is our Military Establishment. Our arms must be mighty, ready for instant action, so that no potential aggressor may be tempted to risk his own destruction.

Our military organization today bears little relation to that known by any of my predecessors in peacetime, or indeed by the fighting men of World War II and Korea.

Until the latest of our world conflicts, the United States had no armaments industry. American makers of plowshares could, with time and as required, make swords as well. But now we can no longer risk emergency improvisation of national defense; we have been compelled to create a permanent armaments industry of vast proportions. Added to this,

3.5 million men and women are directly engaged in the Defense Establishment. We annually spend on military security more than the net income of all United States corporations.

This conjunction of an immense Military Establishment and a large arms industry is new in the American experience. The total influence—economic, political, even spiritual—is felt in every city, every statehouse, every office of the Federal Government. We recognize the imperative need for this development. Yet we must not fail to comprehend its grave implications. Our toil, resources, and livelihood are all involved; so is the very structure of our society.

In the councils of government we must guard against the acquisition of unwarranted influence whether sought or unsought, by the military-industrial complex. The potential for the disastrous rise of misplaced power exists and will persist.

We must never let the weight of this combination endanger our liberties or democratic processes. We should take nothing for granted. Only an alert and knowledgeable citizenry can compel the proper meshing of the huge industrial and military machinery of defense with our peaceful methods and goals so that security and liberty may prosper together.

Akin to and largely responsible for the sweeping changes in our industrial-military posture has been the technological revolution during recent decades. In this revolution research has become central; it also becomes more formalized, complex, and costly. A steadily increasing share is conducted for, by, or at the direction of the Federal Government.

Today the solitary inventor, tinkering in his shop, has been overshadowed by task forces of scientists in laboratories and testing fields. In the same fashion the free university, historically the fountainhead of free ideas and scientific discovery, has experienced a revolution in the conduct of research. Partly because of the huge costs involved, a Government contract becomes virtually a substitute for intellectual curiosity. For every old blackboard there are now hundreds of new electronic computers.

The prospect of domination of the nation's scholars by Federal employment, project allocations, and the power of money is ever present and is gravely to be regarded.

Yet, in holding scientific research and discovery in respect, as we should, we must also be alert to the equal and opposite danger that public policy could itself become the captive of a scientific technological elite.

It is the task of statesmanship to mold, to balance, and to integrate these and other forces, new and old, within the principles of our democratic system—ever aiming toward the supreme goals of our free society.

II. THE MILITARY-INDUSTRIAL COMPLEX
CRITICAL DESCRIPTIONS

EDITOR'S INTRODUCTION

Until President Eisenhower issued his famous warning in the first days of 1961, remarkably little critical attention was publicly paid to the continuously rising defense budget and the apparent increasing absorption by the Defense Department of decision-making powers formerly exercised exclusively by the White House or the State Department. Most citizens had no liking for what was happening, but they were convinced that our defense posture was a necessary response to the Communist menace against which they were repeatedly and vociferously warned. But Eisenhower's Farewell Address raised serious questions. These were seriously examined by informed men trained in the disciplines of social analysis. And the fruits of this examination—bitter fruits, for the most part—were published in what, by the close of the 1960s, had become a large number of technical studies, articles, and books.

A sampling of these is made in this section. Arranged in rough chronological order, they are designed to give a critical view of what the "military-industrial complex" is, how it works, and the dangers which are (to a critical view) inherent in it.

In the opening selection the senator who has done most to bring Pentagon spending under critical public scrutiny, William Proxmire of Wisconsin, chairman of the Subcommittee on Economy in Government of the Joint Economic Committee, reports to Congress (and the American public) the findings of hearings his Subcommittee conducted. The four selections that follow are critical descriptions, from somewhat different points of view, of the way in which Pentagon officials and private contractors work together for the advancement of mutual interests. There follows a case report on the most notorious single "cost overrun" case thus far uncovered, that of the Lockheed C-5A jet project. The section's final two selections have to do with what may become the most important book thus far published about the military-industrial complex, Seymour Melman's *Pentagon Capitalism: The Political Economy of War.*

THE COSTS OF MILITARY SPENDING [1]

When former President Eisenhower left office, he warned against the danger of "unwarranted influences, whether sought or unsought, by the military-industrial complex."

I speak today not to warn against some future danger of this influence. I assert that, whether sought or unsought, there is today unwarranted influence by the military-industrial complex resulting in excessive costs, burgeoning military budgets, and scandalous performances. The danger has long since materialized with a ravaging effect on our nation's spending priorities.

In the first place, we are paying far too much for the military hardware we buy.

But, in addition, and perhaps even more shocking, we often do not get the weapons and products we pay the excessive prices for.

Major components of our weapons systems, for example, routinely do not meet the contract standards and specifications established for them when they are bought. ... A most shocking example of this is to be found in a paper by a Budget Bureau specialist, a very distinguished and able man, Mr. Richard Stubbings, entitled "Improving the Acquisition Process for High Risk Electronics Systems."

Mr. Stubbings shows that in the procurement of some two dozen major weapons systems costing tens of billions of

[1] From "Blank Check for the Military," by Senator William Proxmire (Democrat, Wisconsin), address delivered before United States Senate, March 10, 1969. *Congressional Record.* 115 (daily):5699-703. Mr. 10, '69.

dollars during the 1950s and 1960s, the performance standards of the electronic systems of these weapons seldom met the specifications established for them.

How far they fell below their specifications is a real shock.

Of eleven major weapon systems begun during the 1960s, only two of the eleven electronic components of them performed up to standard. One performed at a 75 per cent level and two at a 50 per cent level. But six—a majority of them—of the eleven performed at a level 25 per cent or less than the standards and specifications set for them.

But that is not all.

Excessive Costs

These systems typically cost 200 to 300 per cent more than the Pentagon estimated.

They were and are delivered two years later than expected.

The after-tax profits of the aerospace industry, of which these contractors were the major companies, were 12.5 per cent higher than for American industry as a whole.

Those firms with the worst records appeared to receive the highest profits. One firm, with failures on five of seven systems, earned 40 per cent more than the rest of the aerospace industry, and 50 per cent more than industry as a whole.

One other company, none of whose seven weapons systems measured up to the performance specifications, had earnings in excess of the industry average. . . .

These revelations raise the most serious questions.

We have high profits without performance.

Rewards are in inverse relationship to the time taken and the funds spent.

Failures are rewarded and minimum standards seldom met. Prices soar. Profits rise. Contracts continue.

This is what I mean when I say that military spending is out of control. This is what I mean when I refer to the "unwarranted influence by the military-industrial complex."

This is what I mean when I assert that we face a condition of excessive costs, burgeoning military budgets, and scandalous performance.

This is why we could get more security for the country by spending smaller amounts, but spending them more effectively.

Some Dangers Ahead

The conditions I have cited above are not only a condition of the 1950s and 1960s. The same dangers lie ahead. . . . The fact is that things may soon become a great deal worse.

One of the ablest men we have had on the financial side of the Government in recent years is Charles Schultze, who was Budget Director under President Johnson for a number of years. Mr. Schultze recently wrote an excellent article in the Brookings Agenda papers, which lists some of the programs now contemplated, authorized, or funded. Among them are:

Minuteman II, which is being improved, and Minuteman III, which is in the offing. Estimated cost: $4.6 billion.

Thirty-one Polaris submarines to be converted to carry 496 Poseidon missiles. Estimated cost: $80 million per submarine, or almost $2.5 billion.

Two hundred and fifty-three new FB-111 bombers. Mr. Schultze does not give the cost estimate.

The thin Sentinel system—the ABM system. Estimated cost was $5 billion. I am now told on excellent authority that it is $10 billion and that this figure does not include funds for the Sprint missiles. If the thin system becomes a "thick" system, the total estimated cost is said to be in the neighborhood of $50 billion. And in a very fascinating analysis the other day by one of the real authorities in Congress on defense, the former Secretary of the Air Force, the Senator from Missouri (Mr. Symington), he estimated that the cost could go as high as $400 billion.

Incidentally, this is a system that even its supporters agree would protect the country for only a limited period of time, perhaps a decade. So that would mean spending $40 billion a year, or half of the total military budget as of now.

Four nuclear-powered carriers. These cost $540 million each, or $2.16 billion.

A new destroyer program. Mr. Schultze does not give the original estimated cost.

Five nuclear-powered escort ships. The cost is estimated at $625 million.

An advanced nuclear attack submarine. Again no cost estimate.

A new navy fighter—VFX-1—to replace the F-111.

Mr. Schultze, and he should know—as I say, he was Budget Director for a number of years, and an outstanding, and brilliant young man—concludes that: One fairly predictable feature of most of these weapons systems is that their ultimate cost will be substantially higher than their currently estimated cost. . . .

That is the understatement of the year. We have seen a doubling in the estimated cost of the Sentinel system alone in a period of one year. And we all know that what the military has hoped to do is to convert it into a "thick" system as a defense against a Soviet as well as a Chinese attack.

Uncritical Approach

What is so discouraging about both the past and the future is the cavalier way in which increases and overruns are shrugged off by the military.

Two billion dollars is a very great amount of money. That is the estimated overrun for only one plane—the C-5A. [See "Report on Lockheed and the C-5A Jet," in this section, below.]

Five billion dollars is a tremendous amount of money. But that is the increase in the estimated cost of the thin Sentinel system in less than a year.

It is virtually impossible to get such funds for housing, jobs, or poverty programs. But the examples I have given are merely the increases and overruns for only two of the many defense weapons systems.

An article published not too long ago in the Washington *Post* indicated the dimensions involved in the matter. It was pointed out that $5 billion, the overrun on the military system, is more than we spend in a year in the entire foreign aid program plus everything we put into housing and urban development. The Pentagon handles it as if it were small change.

What appalls us is the uncritical way in which these increases are accepted by the military. To be consistently wrong on these estimates of cost, as the military has been consistently wrong, should bring the entire system of contracting under the most detailed scrutiny. But there is not the slightest indication that this is being done by the military. In fact, when such questions are raised, we find the services far more defensive than they are eager to improve the system. . . .

Why is the situation so bad? Why is military spending now out of control? Let me give some of the reasons:

First of all, there is far too little critical review at the Pentagon itself. . . . Second . . . [there is a lack of stern and critical review] by the Budget Bureau. . . .

When the new Director of the Budget, Mr. [Robert P.] Mayo, was before the Joint Economic Committee on February 18, I pursued the same subject with him.

The Defense Budget is about $80 billion. Of the remaining budget, according to the Budget Bureau's own analysis, only some $20 billion are "controllable items," that is, items other than interest on the debt, pension and Social Security payments, and so forth, which are relatively fixed and not possible to cut except by major changes in legislation. The military budget of $80 billion, plus that part of the "controllable civilian" budget of $20 billion, together compose about $100 billion which can be critically reviewed. But of the five hundred or so personnel in the Budget Bureau, only about fifty, according to Mr. Mayo, are assigned to scrutinize the Defense budget. This is only 10 per cent of the personnel assigned to the Defense budget.

When I asked Mr. Mayo if at least two to three times as much attention is concentrated on the nondefense, as opposed to the defense, dollars, he said that judged by the allocation of personnel he would not quarrel with the point.

I think it is fair to say, therefore, that the Budget Bureau makes no adequate review of the military budget.

Since the military departments are self-seeking . . . and as the Budget Bureau itself does not scrutinize military spending in anything like the same degree as it examines the budgets of most other departments, this leaves only the Congress and the review we give to military spending as a last defense against excesses and overruns.

I think we would all agree that, while we have very competent and knowledgeable members of both the Armed Services and Appropriation committees, and while they spend a great amount of time and effort on the Defense Department requests, and give as much scrutiny to these matters as it is possible for very busy men and women to give, it is just not possible for Congress to do the detailed job which the Department of Defense and the Budget Bureau should do. . . . We do not have the personnel. We do not have the knowledge. We do not have the time. . . .

There are other reasons why military spending is out of control. . . .

Foremost among these is its sheer size. It is almost impossible for any man or bureau or agency to comprehend, let alone control, $80 billion in funds.

The next most important reason is the lack of competitive bidding and the system of negotiated contracts. This problem is getting worse rather than better.

We have the Defense Department's own figures that formally advertised competitive military contract awards dropped from a far too small 13.4 per cent of total military procurement in fiscal year 1967, to a pathetic 11.5 per cent in fiscal year 1968, or the lowest level since adequate records have been kept.

In addition, the cost plus fixed fee contract has once again increased. It has gone up from a level of about 9 per cent of awards to about 11 per cent, and the Defense Department states that this level may be too low. . . .

Furthermore, given the routine 200 to 300 per cent overrun on most major defense systems, the practice of "buying-in" by firms is promoted and has become notorious.

By "buying-in" I mean a situation where there may be a so-called negotiated procurement in which there are two possible producers at the research and development level. The one who buys in is the one who bids below what he knows it will cost to produce and perhaps takes the business away from the more efficient firm. Once the firm gets it, then watch out, because the overruns, as we have documented again and again, occur. As Secretary Charles testified, those overruns averaged in the past 300 to 700 per cent, so that they have been three to seven times as much as the original bid.

There are a variety of other reasons why expenditures are so excessive.

As Admiral [Hyman G.] Rickover told us, we have no uniform accounting system for defense procurement.

There is an unwillingness of any department ever to admit a mistake.

There is an excessive amount of secrecy which, at times, prevents serious public scrutiny of matters which would benefit from critical review.

There is no really good system of audits while work is underway. Much of the excellent work of the General Accounting Office, by its very nature, is focused on a postaudit review.

But more than all of this, there is what we have come to know as the military-industrial complex and its many ramifications.

The connections between the military, on the one hand, and the major industries which supply it, on the other, are very close and very cooperative. Some of the major companies have dozens of high-ranking retired military personnel on their payrolls.

The major civilian appointive positions at the Department of Defense—the secretaries, under secretaries, and assistant secretaries—are routinely filled by those whose private careers have been with defense industries, key investment houses or banks, or with major law firms which represent the huge industrial complex.

Representatives and senators know only too well the way industry and the military can reach back into states and districts from the howls that go up when any attempt is made to close down even a very inefficient military base in their state or district. We all know the pressures that come upon us to help direct defense projects into our states or districts and the efforts made to keep them there once they have arrived.

The result of all this is a system which is not only inefficient but is now literally out of control.

THE MAKING AND MAKERS OF BUREAUCRATIC TRUTH [2]

The problem of the military power is not unique; it is merely a rather formidable example of the tendency of organization, in an age of organization, to develop a life and purpose and truth of its own. This tendency holds for all great bureaucracies, both public and private. And their action is not what serves a larger public interest, their belief does not reflect the reality of life. What is done and what is believed are, first and naturally, what serve the goals of the bureaucracy itself. Action in the organization interest, or in response to the bureaucratic truth, can thus be a formula for public disservice or even public disaster.

[2] From *How to Control the Military*, by John Kenneth Galbraith, Paul M. Warburg Professor of Economics, Harvard University. Doubleday. '69. p 14-25. Copyright © 1969 by John Kenneth Galbraith. Reprinted by permission of Doubleday & Company, Inc.

There is nothing academic about this possibility. There have been many explanations of how we got into the Vietnam war, an action on which even the greatest of the early enthusiasts have now lapsed into discretion. But all explanations come back to one. It was the result of a long series of steps taken in response to a bureaucratic view of the world—a view to which a President willingly or unwillingly yielded and which, until much too late, was unchecked by any legislative or public opposition. This view was of a planet threatened by an imminent takeover by the unified and masterful forces of the Communist world, directed from Moscow (or later and with less assurance from Peking) and coming to a focus, however improbably, some thousands of miles away in the activities of a few thousand guerrillas against the markedly regressive government of South Vietnam.

The further bureaucratic truths that were developed to support this proposition are especially sobering. What was essentially a civil war between the Vietnamese was converted into an international conflict with rich ideological portent for all mankind. South Vietnamese dictators became incipient Jeffersonians holding aloft the banners of an Asian democracy. Wholesale graft in Saigon became an indispensable aspect of free institutions. An elaborately rigged election became a further portent of democracy. One of the world's most desultory and impermanent armies became, always potentially, a paragon of martial vigor. Airplanes episodically bombing open acreage or dense jungle became an impenetrable barrier to men walking along the ground. An infinity of reverses, losses, and defeats became victories deeply in disguise. Such is the capacity of bureaucracy to create its own truth. . . .

The most spectacular examples of bureaucratic truth are those that serve the military power—and its weapons procurement. . . . These beliefs and their consequences are worth specifying in some detail.

There is first the military belief that whatever the dangers of a continued weapons race with the Soviet Union these

are less than those of any agreement that offers any percep-
tible opening for violation. If there is such an opening the
Soviets will exploit it. Since no agreement can be watertight
this goes far to protect the weapons race from any effort at
control.

Secondly, there is the belief that the conflict with communism is man's ultimate battle. Accordingly, one would not
hesitate to destroy all life if communism seems seriously a
threat. This belief allows acceptance of the arms race no
matter how dangerous. The present ideological differences
between industrial systems will almost certainly look very
different and possibly rather trivial from a perspective of
fifty or a hundred years hence if we survive. Such thoughts
are eccentric.

Third, the national interest is total, that of man inconsequential. So even the prospect of total death and destruction
does not deter us from developing new weapons systems if
some thread of national interest can be identified in the outcome. We can accept 75 million casualties if it forces the
opposition to accept 150 million. This is the unsentimental
calculation. Even more unsentimentally, Senator Richard B.
Russell, the leading Senate spokesman of the military power,
argued on behalf of the army's Sentinel Anti-Ballistic Missile System (ABM) that, if only one man and one woman
are to be left on earth, it was his deep desire that they be
Americans. [The late Senator Russell (Democrat, Georgia)
was chairman of the Armed Services Committee from 1951
until 1969, when he became chairman of the Appropriations
Committee.—Ed.] It was part of the case for the Manned
Orbiting Laboratory (MOL) that it would maintain the
national position in the event of extensive destruction down
below.

Such, not secretly but as they have been articulated, are
the organization truths of the military power. The beliefs
that got us into (and keep us in) Vietnam in their potential
for disaster pale as compared with these doctrines. We shall
obviously have accomplished little if we get out of Vietnam

but leave unchecked in the Government the capacity for this kind of bureaucratic truth. What, in tangible form, is the organization which avows these truths?

It is an organization or a complex of organizations and not a conspiracy. . . . In the conspiratorial view, the military power is a collation of generals and conniving industrialists. The goal is mutual enrichment; they arrange elaborately to feather each other's nest. The industrialists are the *deus ex machina;* their agents make their way around Washington arranging the payoffs. If money is too dangerous, then alcohol, compatible women, more prosaic forms of entertainment or the promise of future jobs to generals and admirals will serve.

There is such enrichment and some graft. Insiders do well. . . . Nonetheless the notion of a conspiracy to enrich and corrupt is gravely damaging to an understanding of the military power. It causes men to look for solutions in issuing regulations, enforcing laws, or sending people to jail. It also, as a practical matter, exaggerates the role of the defense industries in the military power—since they are the people who make the most money, they are assumed to be the ones who, in the manner of the classical capitalist, pull the strings. The armed services are assumed to be in some measure their puppets. The reality is far less dramatic and far more difficult of solution. The reality is a complex of organizations pursuing their sometimes diverse but generally common goals. The participants in these organizations are mostly honest men whose public and private behavior would withstand public scrutiny as well as most. They live on their military pay or their salaries as engineers, scientists, or managers or their pay and profits as executives and would not dream of offering or accepting a bribe.

The organizations that comprise the military power are the four armed services, and especially their procurement branches. And the military power encompasses the specialized defense contractors—General Dynamics, McDonnell

Douglas, Lockheed, or the defense firms of the agglomerates
—of Ling-Temco-Vought or Litton Industries. (About half
of all defense contracts are with firms that do relatively little
other business.) And it embraces the defense divisions of primarily civilian firms such as General Electric or AT&T
[American Telephone & Telegraph Company]. It draws
moral and valuable political support from the unions. Men
serve these organizations in many, if not most, instances, because they believe in what they are doing—because they have
committed themselves to the bureaucratic truth. To find and
scourge a few malefactors is to ignore this far more important commitment.

The military power is not confined to the services and
their contractors—what has come to be called the military-
industrial complex. Associate membership is held by the intelligence agencies which assess Soviet (or Chinese) actions
or intentions. These provide, more often by selection and
bureaucratic belief than by any outright dishonesty, the justification for what the services would like to have and what
their contractors would like to supply. Associated also are
foreign service officers who provide a civilian or diplomatic
gloss to the foreign-policy positions which serve the military
need. The country desks at the State Department, a greatly
experienced former official and ambassador [Ralph Dungan]
has observed, are often "in the hip pocket of the Pentagon—
lock, stock, and barrel, ideologically owned by the Pentagon."

Also a part of the military power are the university scientists and those in such defense-oriented organizations as
RAND, the Institute for Defense Analysis, and Hudson Institute who think professionally about weapons and weapons systems and the strategy of their use. And last, but by no
means least, there is the organized voice of the military in
the Congress, most notably on the Armed Services committees of the Senate and House of Representatives. These are
the organizations which comprise the military power.

The men who comprise these organizations call each other on the phone, meet at committee hearings, serve together on teams or task forces, work in neighboring offices in Washington or San Diego. They naturally make their decisions in accordance with their view of the world—the view of the bureaucracy of which they are a part. The problem is not conspiracy or corruption but unchecked rule. And being unchecked, this rule reflects not the national need but the bureaucratic need—not what is best for the United States but what the air force, army, navy, General Dynamics, North American Rockwell, Grumman Aircraft, State Department representatives, intelligence officers, and Mendel Rivers and Richard Russell believe to be best. [The late L. Mendel Rivers (Democrat, South Carolina), was chairman of the House Armed Services Committee.—Ed.]

THE MANAGERS OF NATIONAL SECURITY [3]

The Economy of Death defies logic. A piece of technology like the ABM is virtually discredited again and again by every former science adviser to the President, a number of Nobel Prize physicists, and several former high officials of the Defense Department itself. Yet the juggernaut moves on. If one rationale for building a new weapons system is exposed as nonsense, others spring up to take its place. The Secretary of State talks about détente and coexistence, and the Secretary of Defense demands the build-up of a first-strike force. The Pentagon demands billions to counter a nonexistent Chinese missile force while ghetto and campus rebellions, police riots, and political assassinations tear away at American society. Why?

The institutions which support the Economy of Death are impervious to ordinary logic or experience because they operate by their own inner logic. Each institutional com-

[3] From *The Economy of Death*, by Richard J. Barnet, codirector of The Institute for Policy Studies, Washington, D.C. Atheneum. '69. p 59 ff. Adapted from *The Economy of Death* by Richard J. Barnet. Copyright © 1969 by Richard J. Barnet. Reprinted by permission of Atheneum Publishers.

ponent of the military-industrial complex has plausible reasons for continuing to exist and expand. Each promotes and protects its own interests and in so doing reinforces the interests of every other. That is what a "complex" is—a set of integrated institutions that act to maximize their collective power. . . . [Let us] look at the various structures of the military-industrial complex to try to understand how and why the decisions are made to allocate our national resources to the Economy of Death. . . .

Nothing suggests the existence of a conspiracy more strongly than concerted efforts . . . [of congressmen, the Department of Defense, and big industrialists] to protect the Military Establishment from public inquiry and debate. But conspiracy is not the answer. The sad truth is that it is not even necessary. To understand the hold of the Economy of Death on the country, one needs to look at the behavior of institutions, not individuals. To be sure, there are more than a few cases of profiteering, personal enrichment, conflict of interest, and graft. Eisenhower's first Secretary of the Air Force, Harold Talbott, who continued to receive over $400,-000 a year from his former company while in office, wrote letters to defense contractors on air force stationery suggesting they might like to throw some business to his old firm. The Senate Permanent Subcommittee on Investigations reported in 1964 that numerous companies "pyramided" profits in connection with the missile procurement program. Western Electric, for example, on a contract for "checking over launcher loaders," earned $955,396 on costs totaling $14,293, a respectable profit of 6600 per cent. Kennedy's Deputy Secretary of Defense, Roswell Gilpatric, played a major role in awarding the dubious TFX contract to his old client General Dynamics. The postwar successors to the merchants of death, such as Litton, Itek, Thiokol, and L-T-V [Ling-Temco-Vought], have earned quick fame and fortune. The present Deputy Secretary of Defense, David Packard, for example, parlayed an electronics shop in a garage into a $300 million personal fortune primarily through defense contracts.

A faint odor of corruption pervades the whole military procurement system. (Some early examples can be found in the House Armed Services Committee Report *Supplemental Hearing Released from Executive Session Relating to Entertainment Furnished by the Martin Company of Baltimore Md. of U.S. Government Officers, September 10, 1959.*) An officer who deals with a defense plant often has access to a variety of personal rewards, including a future with the company. He is likely to eat well, and he need never sleep alone.

But corruption and personal wrongdoing explain very little. In a sense, the managers of the Economy of Death conspire all the time. Men from the services and the defense contractors are constantly putting their heads together to invent ways of spending money for the military. Indeed, that is their job. As John R. Moore, president of North American Rockwell Aerospace and Systems Group, the nation's ninth-ranking defense contractor, puts it, "A new system usually starts with a couple of industry and military people getting together to discuss common problems." Military officers and weapons-pushers from corporations are "interacting continuously at the engineering level," according to Moore. A former Assistant Secretary of Defense who has followed the well-trodden path from the Pentagon to a vice presidency of one of the nation's top military contractors says military procurement is a "seamless web": "Pressures to spend more . . . come from the industry selling new weapons ideas . . . and in part from the military." The problem, then, is not that those who make up the military-industrial complex act improperly, but that they do exactly what the system expects of them. Corruption is not nearly so serious a problem as sincerity. Each part of the complex acts in accordance with its own goals and in so doing reinforces all the others. . . .

Generals and admirals invariably believe that what is good for the air force or the navy is good for America. . . . Each military service has also worked out a view of the world that justifies its own self-proclaimed mission. For the army, the job is to preserve a "balance of power" and to keep order around the world through counterinsurgency campaigns and limited wars. It should be no surprise that the air force view of the world is much more alarmist. . . . It is essential to have an enemy worthy of your own weapons and your own war plans. A strategy based on the nuclear annihilation of the Soviet Union is far easier to accept if that country is the embodiment of evil. To rationalize a nuclear arsenal of 11,000 megaton bombs, it is vital to assume that the leaders in the Kremlin are too depraved to be deterred by less. The anti-Communist reflex is the air force's biggest political asset. . . .

Nevertheless, the uniformed military are not the primary target of a serious political effort to shift from the Economy of Death to the Economy of Life. The principal militarists in America wear three-button suits. They are civilians in everything but outlook. Not the generals but the National Security Managers . . . have been in charge of national-security policy. . . .

Who are the key civilian foreign-policy decision makers? How does one get to be a National Security Manager? Why do they think as they do? . . .

If we take a look at the men who have held the very top positions, the secretaries and under secretaries of State and Defense, the secretaries of the three services, the chairman of the Atomic Energy Commission, and the director of the CIA, we find that out of ninety-one individuals who held these offices during the period 1940-1967, seventy of them were from the ranks of Big Business or high finance, including eight of ten secretaries of Defense, seven out of eight secretaries of the Air Force, every secretary of the Navy, eight out of nine secretaries of the Army, every deputy secretary of Defense, three out of five directors of the CIA, and three out of five chairmen of the Atomic Energy Commission.

The historian Gabriel Kolko investigated 234 top foreign-policy decision makers and found that "men who came from Big Business, investment and law held 59.6 per cent of the posts." The Brookings Institution volume *Men Who*

Govern, a comprehensive study of the top Federal bureau-cracy from 1933 to 1965, reveals that before coming to work in the Pentagon, 86 per cent of the secretaries of the Army, Navy, and Air Force were either businessmen or lawyers (usually with a business practice). In the Kennedy Admin-istration 20 per cent of all civilian executives in defense-related agencies came from defense contractors. . . .

The collection of investment bankers and legal advisers to Big Business who designed the national-security bureau-cracies and helped to run them for a generation came to Washington in 1940. Dr. New Deal was dead, President Roosevelt announced, and Dr. Win-the-War had come to take his place. Two men—Henry L. Stimson, Hoover's Sec-retary of State and a leading member of the Wall Street bar, and James V. Forrestal, president of Dillon Read Company, one of the biggest investment bankers—were responsible for recruiting many of their old friends and associates to run the war. In the formative postwar years of the Truman Ad-ministration, when the essential elements of U.S. foreign and military policy were laid down, these recruits continued to act as the nation's top National Security Managers. Dean Acheson, James V. Forrestal,, Robert Lovett, John McCloy, Averell Harriman, all of whom had become acquainted with foreign policy through running a war, played the crucial roles in deciding how to use America's power in peace.

Once again it was quite natural to look to their own associates, each an American success story, to carry on with the management of the nation's military power. Thus, for example, Forrestal's firm, Dillon Read, contributed Paul Nitze, who headed the State Department Policy Planning Staff in the Truman Administration and ran the Defense Department as deputy to Clark Clifford in the closing year of the Johnson Administration. William Draper, an architect of U.S. postwar policy toward Germany and Japan, came from the same firm. In the Truman years twenty-two key posts in the State Department, ten in the Defense Depart-ment, and five key national-security positions in other agencies were held by bankers who were either Republicans or without party affiliation. As Professor Samuel Huntington has pointed out in his study *The Soldier and the State,* "they possessed all the inherent and real conservatism of the banking breed." Having built their business careers on their judicious management of risk, they now became expert in the management of crisis. Their interests lay in making the system function smoothly—conserving and expanding America's power. They were neither innovators nor problem-solvers. Convinced from their encounter with Hitler that force is the only thing that pays off in international relations, they all operated on the assumption that the endless stockpiling of weapons was the price of safety.

The Eisenhower Administration tended to recruit its National Security Managers from the top manufacturing corporations rather than from the investment banking houses. To be sure, bankers were not exactly unwelcome in the Eisenhower years. Robert Cutler, twice the President's Special Assistant for National Security Affairs, was chairman of the board of the Old Colony Trust Company in Boston; Joseph Dodge, the influential director of the Bureau of the Budget, was a Detroit banker; Douglas Dillon, of Dillon Read, was Under Secretary of State for Economic Affairs; Thomas Gates, the last Eisenhower Secretary of Defense, was a Philadelphia banker and subsequently head of the Morgan Guaranty Trust Company.

But most of the principal figures of the era were associated with the leading industrial corporations, either as chief executives or directors; many of these corporations ranked among the top one hundred defense contractors. Eisenhower's first Secretary of Defense was Charles Wilson, president of General Motors; his second was Neil McElroy, a public-relations specialist who became president of Procter and Gamble. One Deputy Secretary of Defense was Robert B. Anderson, a Texas oilman. Another was Roger Kyes, another General Motors executive, and a third was Donald Quarles of Westinghouse. . . .

When President Kennedy was elected on his campaign promise to "get the country moving again," the first thing he did was to reach back eight years for advice on national security. Many of the men he appointed as top National Security Managers of the New Frontier were the old faces of the Truman Administration. In addition to Dean Rusk, a strong MacArthur supporter in the Korean war who wrote the memorandum urging that UN forces cross the 38th Parallel in Korea, Kennedy's State Department appointments also included George McGhee, a successful oil prospector and principal architect of Truman's Middle East policy. Adolph Berle, Averell Harriman, Paul Nitze, John McCone, John McCloy, William C. Foster, and other experienced hands from the national-security world also made it clear that the new Administration would follow familiar patterns.

However, the Kennedy Administration brought in some new faces, too. McGeorge Bundy, the Dean of the Faculty of Arts and Sciences at Harvard when Kennedy was an overseer, impressed the new President with his crisp, concise, and conventional analysis. The son of Henry Stimson's close wartime assistant, the Boston trust lawyer Harvey H. Bundy, McGeorge was a publicist who had put the Stimson papers in order and published a highly laudatory edition of Acheson's speeches while the Secretary (the father-in-law of Bundy's brother William) was under attack in the Congress. The teacher of a highly popular undergraduate course on power and international relations, Bundy appeared to have all the necessary qualifications to be the Special Assistant for National Security Affairs. Walt Rostow, the energetic MIT professor who, in his own words, had not spent a year outside of the Government since 1946, was . . . made Bundy's assistant.

Into the Defense Department also came a contingent of systems analysts and nuclear strategists from the RAND Corporation. These were not exactly new faces either. During the Eisenhower years they had been in and out of Washington, prodding the military services into more innovative thinking, which usually meant buying new hardware. Now they became the bosses of the men they had been advising. Charles Hitch, the RAND economist who had written a book on cost effectiveness in defense spending, was invited to put his program-packaging notions into effect as comptroller of the Defense Department. With Hitch came Alain Enthoven, Harry Rowan, and other RAND alumni, who became known as the "whiz kids."

However, the principal positions, with the exception of Bundy's, were filled according to the old patterns. Robert McNamara was president of Ford instead of General Motors; Roswell Gilpatric, appointed Deputy Secretary of Defense, was a partner of a leading Wall Street firm. In career experience he differed from his immediate Republican predecessor, James Douglas, in three principal respects. His law office was in New York rather than Chicago. He had been Under Secretary of the Air Force, while Douglas had been Secretary. He was a director of Eastern Airlines instead of American Airlines.

The Johnson Administration continued most of the Kennedy national-security appointments. . . .

The Nixon Administration brought in a veteran academic foreign-policy analyst, two business lawyers, one of the leading defenders of the military in the House, and one of California's most successful defense contractors to decide the national interest. Henry Kissinger [Assistant to the President for National Security Affairs], the academic, had made his reputation by advocating the judicious use of so-called "tactical" nuclear weapons on the battlefield. He then enhanced it by retracting his inherently mad proposal, thus demonstrating flexibility. The business lawyers, [Secretary of State] William Rogers and Elliot Richardson, had had no previous national-security or foreign-policy experience. . . . [Richardson has since become Secretary of Health, Education, and Welfare.—Ed.] The Congressman Melvin Laird [appointed Secretary of Defense by President Nixon in 1969] had an uncanny faculty for seeing all sorts of gaps in America's "security posture" and had written a book recommending that the United States launch a nuclear strike against the Soviet Union if "the Communist empire further moves to threaten the peace."

The National Security Managers, like the uninformed military, have looked at the world through very special lenses, and the result has been a remarkable consensus. . . .

[They] have not regarded the redistribution of wealth as a priority concern, for they have had neither the experience nor the incentive to understand the problems of the poor. . . . For a National Security Manager recruited from the world of business, there are no other important constituencies to which he feels a need to respond.

When planning a decision on defense policy, he does not solicit the views of civil-rights leaders, farmers, laborers, mayors, artists, or small businessmen. Nor do people from these areas of national life become National Security Managers. Indeed, when Martin Luther King expressed opposition to the Vietnam war, he was told that it was "inappropriate" for someone in the civil-rights movement to voice his views on foreign policy. The opinions which the National Security Manager values are those of his friends and colleagues. They have power, which is often an acceptable substitute for judgment, and since they view the world much as he does, they must be right. They are also the men with whom he will most likely have to deal when he lays down the burdens of office. "What will my friends on Wall Street say?" the director of the Arms Control and Disarmament Agency once exclaimed when asked to endorse a disarmament proposal that would limit the future production of missiles.

The idea that spending one's life in the securities market is an essential qualification for dealing in national security is a confusion. There is no reason why the National Security Managers should not represent diverse interests, backgrounds, and ways of looking at the national interest. It is almost unbelievable that of the four hundred top decision makers who have assumed the responsibility for the survival of the species, only one has been a woman. [Mrs. Anna M. Rosenberg, Assistant Secretary of Defense 1951-1953.]

MILITARY PROCUREMENT [4]

Military and military-related spending accounts for about 45 per cent of all Federal expenditures. In fiscal 1968, the total Federal outlays were $178.9 billion. The Defense Department alone spent $77.4 billion, and such related programs as military assistance to foreign countries, atomic energy and the Selective Service System raised the figure to $80.5 billion. The $4 billion program of the National Aeronautics and Space Administration and other activities intertwined with the military carry the real level of defense spending considerably higher.

To place the defense bill in perspective we should note that 1968 appropriations were less than $500 million for food stamps, school lunches and the special milk program combined. For all federally assisted housing programs, including Model Cities, they were about $2 billion. The poverty program received less than $2 billion. Federal aid to education was allotted about $5.2 billion. The funds spent on these programs and all those categorized as health, education, welfare, housing, agriculture, conservation, labor, commerce, foreign aid, law enforcement, etc.—in short, all civilian programs—amounted to about $82.5 billion, if the space and veterans' programs are not included, and less than $70 billion if the interest on the national debt is not considered.

[4] From "We Must Guard Against Unwarranted Influence by the Military-Industrial Complex," by Richard F. Kaufman. New York *Times Magazine*. p 10-11+. Je. 22, '69. © 1969 by The New York Times Company. Reprinted by permission. Mr. Kaufman is an economist on the staff of the Subcommittee on Economy in Government of the United States Congress' Joint Economic Committee chaired by Senator William Proxmire.

The largest single item in the military budget—it accounted for $44 billion in 1968—is procurement, which in-
cludes purchasing, renting or leasing supplies and services
(and all the machinery for drawing up and administering
the contracts under which those purchases and rentals are
made). Procurement, in other words, means Government
contracts; it is mother's milk to the military-industrial complex.

The Pentagon annually signs agreements with about
22,000 prime contractors; in addition, more than 100,000
subcontractors are involved in defense production. Defense-
oriented industry as a whole employs about 4 million men.
However, although a large number of contractors do some
military business, the largest share of procurement funds is
concentrated among a relative handful of major contractors.
Last year the 100 largest defense suppliers obtained $26.2
billion in military contracts. . . .

Similarly, the Atomic Energy Commission's contract
awards tend to be concentrated in a select group of major
corporations. Of approximately $1.6 billion awarded in con-
tracts last year, all but $104 million went to 36 contractors.
As for NASA, procurement plays a larger role in its activities
than in those of any other Federal agency. More than 90
per cent of its funds are awarded in contracts to industry
and educational institutions. Of the $4.1 billion worth of
procurement last year, 92 per cent of the direct awards to
business went to NASA's one hundred largest contractors.

In terms of property holdings, the result of almost two
centuries of military procurement is a worldwide and practically incalculable empire. An almost arbitrary and greatly
underestimated value—$202.5 billion—was placed on mili-
tary real and personal property at the end of fiscal year 1968.
Weapons were valued at $100 billion. Supplies and plant
equipment accounted for $55.6 billion. Most of the re-
mainder was in real estate. The Pentagon says the 29 million
acres it controls—an area almost the size of New York State—
are worth $38.7 billion. (The official Defense Department

totals do not include 9.7 million acres, valued at $9 billion, under the control of the Army Civil Works Division or additional property valued at $4.7 billion.) The arbitrariness of those figures is seen in the fact that they represent *acquisition* costs. Some of the military real estate was acquired more than a century ago, and much of it is in major cities and metropolitan areas. The actual value of the real estate must be many times its acquisition cost.

But the important fact about procurement is not the extent of the Pentagon's property holdings; it is that defense contracting has involved the military with many of the largest industrial corporations in America. Some companies do almost all their business with the Government. Into this category fall a number of the large aerospace concerns—such giants as General Dynamics, Lockheed Aircraft and United Aircraft. For such other companies as General Electric, AT&T [American Telephone & Telegraph Company] and General Motors, Government work amounts to only a small percentage of the total business. But the tendency is for a company to enlarge its share of defense work over the years, at least in dollar value. And whether defense contracts represent 5 per cent or 50 per cent of a corporation's annual sales, they become a solid part of the business, an advantage to maintain or improve upon. A company may even work harder to increase its military sales than it does to build commercial sales because military work is more profitable, less competitive, more susceptible to control through lobbying in Washington. The industrial giants with assets of more than $1 billion have swarmed around the Pentagon to get their share of the sweets with no less enthusiasm than their smaller brethren.

The enormous attraction of military and military-related contracts for the upper tiers of industry has deepened in the last few years as military procurement has increased sharply. For example, GE's prime-contract awards have gone up from $783 million in 1958 to $1.5 billion in 1968; General Motors went from $281 million in 1958 to $630 million in 1968.

While much of this increase can be traced to the Vietnam war boom and many contractors would suffer a loss of business if the war ended, there was steady growth in the defense industry during the fifties and early sixties. . . .

What seems to be happening is that defense production is gradually spreading throughout industry, although the great bulk of the funds is still spent among relatively few companies. Still, as the defense budget increases the procurement dollars go further. The geographical concentration of defense production in the industrialized, high-income states also suggests that military contracts have come less and less to be restricted to an isolated sector of the economy specializing in guns and ammunition. Military business has become solidly entrenched in industrial America.

Considering the high degree of mismanagement and inefficiency in defense production and the tendency for contractors to want more sales and therefore to support the military in its yearly demands for a larger budget, this is not a healthy situation. The inefficiency of defense production, particularly in the aerospace industry, can hardly be disputed. Richard A. Stubbing, a defense analyst at the Bureau of the Budget, in a study of the performance of complex weapon systems . . . found that in thirteen aircraft and missile programs produced since 1955 at a total cost of $40 billion, fewer than 40 per cent of the electronic components performed acceptably; two programs were canceled at a cost to the Government of $2 billion, and two programs costing $10 billion were phased out after three years because of low reliability.

And the defense industry is inefficient as well as unreliable. Albert Shapero, professor of management at the University of Texas, has accused aerospace contractors of habitually overstaffing, overanalyzing and overmanaging. A. E. Fitzgerald, a Deputy Assistant Secretary of the Air Force, in testimony before the Joint Economic [Committee's] Subcommittee on Economy in Government, described poor work habits and poor discipline in contractors' plants. In the same hearing, a retired Air Force officer, Colonel A. W. Buesking, a former director of management systems control in the office of the Assistant Secretary of Defense, summarized a study he had conducted by saying that control systems essential to prevent excessive costs simply did not exist.

In a sense, industry is being seduced into bad habits of production and political allegiance with the lure of easy money. And industry is not the only sector being taken in. Consider conscription (3.6 million men in uniform), the Pentagon's civilian bureaucracy (1.3 million), the work force in defense-oriented industry (4 million), the domestic brain drain created by the growth in military technology, the heavy emphasis on military research and development as a percentage (50 per cent) of all American research, the diversion of universities to serve the military and defense industry. These indicators reveal a steady infiltration of American values by those of the Military Establishment: production for nonproductive use, compulsory service to the state, preparation for war. In the process, the economy continues to lose many of the attributes of the marketplace. In the defense industry, for all practical purposes, there is no marketplace.

The general rule for Government procurement is that purchases shall be made through written competitive bids obtained by advertising for the items needed. In World War II the competitive-bid requirements were suspended. After the war the Armed Services Procurement Act was passed, restating the general rule but setting out seventeen exceptions—circumstances under which negotiation would be authorized instead of competition. The exceptions, which are still in use, are very broad and very vague. If the item is determined to be critical or complex or if delivery is urgent or if few supplies exist and competition is impractical or if emergency conditions exist or if security considerations preclude advertising, the Pentagon can negotiate for what it wants. . . .

Last year [1968] about 90 per cent of the Pentagon's and 98 per cent of NASA's contract awards were negotiated under the "exceptions."

What this means is that there is no longer any objective criterion for measuring the fairness of contract awards. Perhaps more important, control over the costs, quality and time of production, insofar as they resulted from competition, are also lost. Negotiation involves informal discussion between the Pentagon and its contractors over the price and other terms of the contract. It permits subjective decision making on such important questions as which firms to do business with and what price to accept. The Pentagon can negotiate with a single contractor, a "sole source," or it can ask two or three to submit proposals. . . .

Typically, the Pentagon will invite a few of the large contractors to submit proposals for a contract to perform the research and development on a new weapon system. The one who wins occupies a strategic position. The know-how he gains in his research work gives him an advantage over his rivals for the larger and more profitable part of the program, the production. This is what is meant when it is said that the Government is "locked in" with a contractor. Because the contractor knows he will obtain a lock-in if he can do the initial research work, there is a tendency to stretch a few facts during the negotiations.

Contractor performance is measured by three factors: the total cost to the Government of the weapon system, the way in which it functions and the time of delivery. During the contract negotiations over these factors the phenomenon known as the "buy-in" may occur. The contractor, in order to "buy in" to the program, offers more than he can deliver. He may promise to do a job at a lower cost than he knows will be incurred or to meet or exceed performance specifications that he knows are unattainable or to deliver the finished product long before he has reason to believe it will be ready.

Technically, the contractor can be penalized for his failure to fulfill promises made during the negotiations, but the Government rarely insists on full performance. The contractor knows this, of course, and he also knows the "get-well" stratagem. That is, he can reasonably expect, on practically all major weapon contracts, that should he get into difficulty with regard to any of the contract conditions, the Government will extricate him—get him well.

The contractor can get well in a variety of ways. If his costs run higher than his estimates, the Pentagon can agree to pay them. (Cost increases can be hidden through contract-change notices. On a typical, complex weapon system, the changes from original specifications will number in the thousands; some originate with the Pentagon, some are authorized at the request of the contractor. The opportunities for burying real or phony cost increases are obvious, so much so that in defense circles contract-change notices are sometimes referred to as "contract nourishment.") The Government can also accept a weapon that performs poorly or justify a late delivery. If for some reason it is impossible for the Pentagon to accept a weapon, there is still a way to keep the contractor well. The Pentagon can cancel a weapon program for the "convenience" of the Government. A company whose contract is canceled for default stands to lose a great deal of money, but cancellation for convenience reduces or eliminates the loss; the Government makes reimbursement for costs incurred. An example of this occurred recently in connection with the F-111B, the navy's fighter-bomber version of the TFX.

Gordon W. Rule, a civilian procurement official who had responsibility for the F-111B, said in testimony before the House Subcommittee on Military Operations that General Dynamics was in default on its contract because the planes were too heavy to meet the height or range requirements. Rule proposed in a memorandum to Deputy Secretary of Defense Paul H. Nitze that the contract be terminated for default. At the same time, Assistant Secretary of the Air Force Robert H. Charles and Roger Lewis the General Dynamics chairman, proposed that the navy reimburse the company for all costs and impose no penalty. Nitze's compromise was to make reimbursement of $216.5 million, mostly to General Dynamics, and to impose a small penalty.

In a memo written last year Rule made this comment on the attitude of defense contractors: "No matter how poor the quality, how late the product and how high the cost, they know nothing will happen to them."

There are many other ways to succeed in the defense business without really trying. The Pentagon generously provides capital to its contractors; more than $13 billion worth of Government-owned property, including land, buildings and equipment, is in contractors' hands. In addition, the Pentagon will reimburse a supplier during the life of his contract for as much as 90 per cent of the costs he reports. These are called "progress" payments, but are unrelated to progress in the sense of contract objectives achieved; they correspond only to the costs incurred. The progress payments are interest-free loans that provide the contractor with working capital in addition to fixed capital. They minimize his investment in the defense business and free his assets for commercial work or for obtaining new defense work.

Investigations by the General Accounting Office have revealed that the Government's money and property have been used by contractors for their own purposes. . . . [A] recent incident involved Thiokol Chemical Corporation, Aerojet-General (a subsidiary of General Tire & Rubber Company) and Hercules, Inc. From 1964 through 1967 they received a total of $22.4 million to be used for work on the Air Force Minuteman missile program. The Government accountants found that the three contractors misused more than $18 million of this money, spending it for research unrelated and inapplicable to Minuteman or any other defense program.

The defense industry is perhaps the most heavily subsidized in the nation's history. Thanks to Pentagon procurement policies, large contractors find their defense business to be their most lucrative. Although no comprehensive study of such profits has been made, the known facts indicate that profits on defense contracts are higher than those on related nondefense business, that they are higher for the defense industry than for manufacturing as a whole and that the differential has been increasing. In a study that compared the five-year period from 1959 through 1963 with the last six months of 1966, the General Accounting Office found a 26 per cent increase in the average profit rates negotiated. Admiral Hyman G. Rickover has testified that suppliers of propulsion turbines are insisting on profits of 20 to 25 per cent, compared with 10 per cent a few years ago, and that profits on ship-building contracts have doubled in two years.

The figures cited by Rickover relate to profits as a percentage of costs, a measure that often understates the true profit level. The more accurate measure is return on investment. An example of the difference was demonstrated in a 1962 tax-court case, *North American Aviation* v. *Renegotiation Board*. The contracts provided for 8 per cent profits as a percentage of costs; the tax court found that the company had realized profits of 612 per cent and 802 per cent on its investment in two succeeding years. The reason for the huge return on investment was the Defense Department policy of supplying both fixed and working capital to many of the larger contractors. In some cases the amount of Government-owned property exceeds the contractor's investment, which is sometimes minimal. It is no wonder that contractors prefer to talk about profits as a percentage of costs.

Murray Weidenbaum, recently appointed Assistant Secretary of the Navy, found in a study that between 1962 and 1965 a sample of large defense contractors earned 17.5 per cent net profit (measured as a return on investment), while companies of similar size doing business in the commercial market earned 10.6 per cent.

The Pentagon has attempted to answer the critics of high defense profits by citing the findings of the Logistics Management Institute, a think tank that has done a study showing declining defense profits. The trouble with the institute's study is that it used unverified, unaudited data obtained on a voluntary basis from a sample of defense contractors. Those who did not want to participate simply did not return the questionnaires; in fact, 42 per cent of those contacted provided no data. There is no way of knowing whether the group of contractors who refused to participate in the study included the ones making the highest profits.

There is almost no risk in defense contracting except that borne by the Government. If a major prime contractor has ever suffered a substantial loss on a defense contract, the Pentagon has failed to disclose his name, although it has been requested to do so by members of Congress. On the other hand, the disputed Cheyenne helicopter and C-5A cargo plane projects could conceivably result in large losses for Lockheed, the contractor in both cases. Lockheed asserts that it might still make a profit on the C-5A (which is being produced in a Government-owned plant), and denies that it is at fault in the cancellation of production on the Cheyenne helicopter (on which research work has been resumed). Past experience suggests that one should await the final decision, which may be two years in coming, before making flat statements about profit and loss. [For a detailed account of Lockheed's troubles see "Report on Lockheed and the C-5A Jet," in this section, below.—Ed.]

THE WEAPONS MAKERS [5]

If one is looking for the hard core of the military-industrial complex, it isn't difficult to find. It's in the areospace industries that have crowded out the orange groves in California, growing fat in the beneficent artificial stimulation of the Pentagon's fiscal sun. Here we find the missile makers, the producers of aircraft, and the electronics manufacturers who depend upon the Pentagon for their business. In some companies like Lockheed and General Dynamics, the United

[5] From *Arms Beyond Doubt*, by Ralph E. Lapp. Cowles. '70. p 144-7, 153-60, 170-2. Copyright 1970 by Ralph E. Lapp. Published by arrangement with Cowles Book Company, Inc. Dr. Lapp is a physicist and expert on weapons technology. He was division director of the Manhattan Project which created the first A-bombs, former scientific adviser to the Pentagon, and former executive director for atomic energy of the Defense Department's Research and Development Board.

States Government represents the single customer and there-in lies the conundrum of the military-industrial complex.

General Dynamics, for example, is the top defense con-tractor with $2.24 billion in sales to the Defense Department, accounting for 85 per cent of its total sales. Lockheed, with annual sales of $1.87 billion to the Pentagon, is in much the same position. These two companies account for one tenth of the defense prime military contract awards each year. The top twelve largest defense contractors account for one third of the dollar value of all contract awards.

Quite evidently, the making of weapons is big business—American style. This is really new to our peacetime way of life, since between wars the United States put a low priority on military preparedness. In fact, defense budgets after World War II dipped to a $13 billion annual low—a figure that prevailed until the Korean war.

Korea shot military expenditures above the $40 billion mark. At the same time, something new happened in the mili-tary scheme of things—the United States began the peacetime mobilization of its science and technology. Spurred by Korea, the technological arms race had begun. Thereafter, the Pen-tagon's budget exhibited increasing commitments to research and development that was dedicated to evolving new weapons of war.

When President Eisenhower took office, the defense R&D [Research and Development] budget topped $2.5 billion and more than doubled by the time he gave his famous farewell address on the military-industrial complex. It was not only the manufacture of weapons that was big business; research and development of military hardware became a major source of income for thousands of U.S. corporations, nonprofit insti-tutions, and universities, as well.

The extent of the U.S. dedication to weapon development is revealed by a single statistic. The Defense Department and the Atomic Energy Commission spent in excess of $100 billion on research and development in the twelve-year period ending in 1970. During the same time span, only about one tenth this amount of money was spent on the support of basic science by the National Science Foundation and on health research by the Department of Health, Education, and Welfare. The nation's priorities were aimed squarely in the direction of national defense.

The big business aspect of defense research is illustrated by data taken from the Defense Department's latest report of the five hundred contractors performing research, development, test, and engineering work under prime military contracts. In fiscal year 1968 we find the top ten contractors were as follows:

Prime Military Contractor	Total Contract Dollars
1. Lockheed Aircraft Corp.	$918.8 million
2. General Electric Co.	573.1
3. Western Electric Co.	482.2
4. General Dynamics Corp.	429.1
5. North American-Rockwell Corp.	298.2
6. McDonnell Douglas Corp.	224.4
7. Boeing Co.	220.6
8. Martin Marietta Corp.	172.0
9. Hughes Aircraft Co.	139.7
10. Massachusetts Institute of Technology	124.1
	$3,582.2 million

If the layman thinks that private enterprise puts up its own money to develop new defense technology, he will be shocked to learn that this is a myth. For example, in the decade beginning 1957 the total amount of money spent on research and development in the aircraft and missiles industry was $40 billion. Of this private industry put up only $4.45 billion or 11 per cent of the total.

In general, the nation's largest R&D contractors also head the list of those receiving the largest prime military contracts for production. Research and development is even more concentrated among the largest corporations than is production of military equipment—the top nine R&D firms account for almost half the total R&D dollars. According to the Pentagon's Directorate for Statistical Services, 85 per cent of the research and development work is connected with missile, space, aircraft, and electronics programs. This substantiates the author's contention that the hard core of the military-industrial complex is the aerospace industry.

Among the nation's five hundred largest R&D contractors for the Pentagon are numbered ninety-one universities and numerous university-associated institutes. The U.S. National Academy of Sciences is listed as receiving $2.84 million in military contracts awarded by the Defense Department. Numbers of contracts and their dollar amounts are sometimes less impressive than the nature of the research being funded.

For example, Senator Gaylord Nelson [Democrat] of Wisconsin introduced into the *Congressional Record* (page S 9495 on August 8, 1969) a list of more than fifty universities "engaged in highly secret and dangerous chemical-biological research." He identified the research by listing ninety specific contract numbers for work at the universities and their medical schools.

The Pentagon's support of research on campus was initially concentrated in the area of the "hard" sciences, especially in physics and chemistry, but it soon expanded into many other areas, including the "soft" social sciences.

The U.S. Army, for example, entered into a contractual agreement with American University in Washington, D.C., to study the subjects of counterrevolution and counterinsurgency in Latin America. The National Academy of Sciences became involved in this work, known as Project Camelot, but subsequently washed its hands of the whole business.

The $6 million army project ran into real difficulties as its true nature percolated through to conscience-stricken members of the academic community. In a postmortem, conducted after Camelot was canceled, Professor Irving Horowitz of Washington University observed: "From the outset, there seems to have been a 'gentleman's agreement' not to inquire or interfere in Project Camelot, but simply to serve as some sort of camouflage." Professor Horowitz found that the army-university relationship was not one of equals. He pointed to Project Camelot as a "tragic precedent" and concluded:

> It reflects the arrogance of a consumer of intellectual merchandise. And this relationship of inequality corrupted the lines of authority, and profoundly limited the autonomy of the social scientists involved. It became clear that the social scientist savant was not so much functioning as an applied social scientist as he was supplying information to a powerful client.

The independence of a university should be cherished by a democracy because it bears a special relationship to the vitality of a nation's free spirit and intellectual integrity. This is of cardinal importance when the flood of Federal dollars poses such a potential corrupting influence on campus. . . .

Bernard D. Nossiter, an astute reporter for the Washington *Post,* looked into the aerospace plans for the future and managed to gain access to the plans of several firms. L-T-V Aerospace Corporation, for example, opened its "Blue Book" to him. This book projects L-T-V's growth for the next five years. . . .

L-T-V shot up from position number sixty-one on the list of largest defense contractors to number seven during the 1961-69 time period. Nossiter learned that it has patterned its future on rising even higher on the list, hoping for $1.1 billion in defense work by 1973. The aerospace corporation owns only about 1 per cent of the 6.7 million square feet of office-laboratory-factory space it uses for defense work; the remainder is Government-owned.

In an exclusive interview with Samuel F. Downer, financial vice president of L-T-V Aerospace, the reporter managed to bring out into the open some of the company's philosophy on defense sales and their connection to politics. Downer expounded on this subject as follows:

> It's basic. Its selling appeal is defense of the home. This is one of the greatest appeals the politicians have in adjusting the system. If you're the President and you need a control factor in the economy, and you need to sell this factor, you can't sell Harlem and Watts but you can sell self-preservation, a new environment. We're going to increase defense budgets as long as those bastards in Russia are ahead of us.

Such corporate candor is chilling. If this is the attitude of other aerospace concerns, then is not the military-industrial complex cast in a rather sinister light? Will U.S. corporations be content to perform a purely passive role of providing requested services to the Defense Department? Or, in the course of seeking corporate growth, may they not assume a promotional attitude? We know that huge corporations maintain highly organized public relations departments, capable of disseminating propaganda on a broad scale. When aerospace firms buy full-page color ads in national magazines glorifying their products, they promote not just their companies but also the Cold War.

The real danger exists that aerospace industries, faced with cutbacks, will seek to create a climate in which the Pentagon's budget is increased. To understand that this is a serious possibility, we need to trace the economic fortunes of the aerospace industry up to the present time. In this way we may be able to sense the predicament in which the aerospace industries find themselves.

During the 1960s aerospace sales followed the pattern illustrated by the table given below:

U.S. Aerospace Sales (1960-1969)

	U.S. Government*	Total Sales†
1960	$13.6 billion	$17.3 billion
1961	14.4	18.9
1962	15.6	19.1
1963	16.8	20.1
1964	16.8	20.5
1965	16.9	21.7
1966	18.3	24.3
1967	19.7	26.2
1968	22.0	29.8
1969 est	23.0	28.3

* Sales to Defense Department and to National Aeronautics and Space Administration and other Federal agencies. Does not include nonaerospace items.
† Includes non-Government and nonaerospace items.

It is apparent from this summary that the aerospace industries have shown growth as a result of doing business primarily with the Federal Government. In the decade of the sixties, NASA [National Aeronautics and Space Administration] accounted for $32 billion of aerospace sales and the Pentagon's total exceeded $150 billion. Up to 1965, the NASA contribution served to keep the sales curve from dipping, which it would have done because Secretary [Robert S.] McNamara [former Secretary of Defense] clamped restrictions on defense spending in this sector and had programmed further reductions through the second half of the decade.

In 1965 the aerospace industries were in trouble. The booster effect of Project Apollo was wearing off and Secretary McNamara's cutbacks were such that, barring other developments, Government sales would be below their 1960 level.

Of course, something did happen to change this gloomy picture. The war in Vietnam provided the economic adrenalin for aerospace sales. However, as one looks back at this decade-long record of sales, the conclusion seems inescapable —except for Vietnam and Apollo, the aerospace industries did not belong in the "growth" category.

In 1970 this complex of companies is again in trouble. Apollo has been successful, but for NASA the price of success was bitter—the prospect of a reduced budget. The tapering off of the war in Vietnam threatens to dry up the flood of aircraft orders and the congressional crackdown on the Pentagon's budget has eliminated such items as the $3.2 billion Manned Orbiting Laboratory and the Cheyenne helicopter. Moreover, the F-111 program has been pruned back by eliminating the navy's version of this plane. All of which goes to explain why the Wall Street analysts have rated aerospace stocks in such a dismal manner.

When asked about his company's future prospects by a *Christian Science Monitor* reporter, Roger Lewis, president and board chairman of General Dynamics, replied:

> If circumstances do permit smaller military forces in the future and, therefore, a small volume of defense production, this would mean to me only an even more competitive atmosphere in which General Dynamics would work even harder to maintain a high-win rate in defense contracts.

Lewis referred to this as a "thinning out" process whereby a fewer number of companies would share the largest part of weapons development and production. However, he seeks to perpetuate the myth of competitive awards of defense contracts. The majority of defense contracts fall into the "negotiated" category and many into the "single source" cubicle.

Even when it appears that a contract is awarded on a competitive basis, one must look closely at the procedures followed. It is not unusual for a firm to be almost guaranteed a production contract if it wins a research and development award. The latter gives the R&D performer a unique advantage since it is the single parent of the evolving product. Pentagon-impregnated, the defense contractor is most likely to keep the "child" from the earliest growth stage through to maturity.

Testifying on the military-industrial complex before the [United States Congress] Joint Economic Committee, Professor Galbraith made the following observations about the Government-contractor relationship in defense business:

I, myself, have argued that with industrial development—with advanced technology, high organization, large and rigid commitments of capital—power tends to pass to the producing organization—to the modern large corporation.

. . . All things considered, I feel that the aerospace complex represents an island of defense socialism within the national economy. . . . The fact is that . . . [the aerospace contractors] bear only a faint resemblance to private enterprise in their dealings with the Department of Defense.

There are, in addition, aspects of the military-industrial complex that we have not yet considered. These include, first, the interlocking personaliies that shuttle in and out of the various domains of the complex; second, the monumental cost overruns made in performance of defense contracts; and, finally, the mammoth mistakes made by both the military and industrial components of the complex.

In the spring of 1969 Senator Proxmire disclosed that one hundred of the largest defense contractors, responding to a senatorial inquiry, employed 2,072 retired military officers of the rank of colonel or navy captain and above. The Wisconsin senator introduced into the *Congressional Record* for March 24, 1969, the . . . table [on the facing page] showing the employment of high-ranking retired military officers. . . .

The Proxmire study revealed that the number of retired high-ranking military officers employed by defense industry had tripled in the past decade. Industry has shown a tendency to hire top level ex-military men, including officers of very high rank—up to lieutenant general level. For example, Lockheed Aircraft employs two air force lieutenant generals and one army officer of the same rank. North American-Rockwell lists three vice presidents of general rank.

Rank	Company	Number Employed Feb. 1, 1969	Defense Contracts Fiscal Year 1968
1.	Lockheed Aircraft Corp.	210	$1,870,000,000
2.	Boeing Co.	169	762,000,000
3.	McDonnell Douglas Corp.	141	1,101,000,000
4.	General Dynamics	113	2,239,000,000
5.	North American-Rockwell	104	669,000,000
6.	General Electric Co.	89	1,489,000,000
7.	Ling-Temco-Vought, Inc.	69	758,000,000
8.	Westinghouse Electric Corp.	59	251,000,000
9.	TRW, Inc.	56	127,000,000
10.	Hughes Aircraft Co.	55	286,000,000

Putting retired military men on a company's payroll is no crime. Many colonels or officers of equivalent and lower rank acquire considerable technical expertise in their years of military service. It would be wasteful for the nation not to tap such a skilled reservoir of talent. However, the potential for misuse of retired military men lies in their employment for purposes of influencing defense officials in contractual negotiations and in the obtaining of privileged information about weapons systems. The basic issue is one of conflict of interest and influence. [See "The Costs of Military Spending," in this section, above, an excerpt from Senator Proxmire's speech of March 10, 1969, on the Senate floor.]

The problem is not limited to uniformed officers of the three services—as Senator Proxmire concluded in a letter dated June 23, 1969, addressed to Attorney General John N. Mitchell:

When Government contracting officers and representatives— whether civilian or military—leave the Government and go to work directly for a company where they have just been representing the Government on contracts with that company, there certainly appears to be a *prima facie* case of serious conflict of interest.

The Senator's letter contained specific reference to such a conflict of interest in the case of four air force officials and one general hired by North American-Rockwell's Autonetic Division.

The mass migration of high-ranking retired officers and officials from defense positions to jobs with private industry certainly invites the suspicion that impropriety may be involved. But this is by no means confined to a Pentagon emigration. It also involves the shuttling into and out of Washington of civilians from private industry or from institutions of higher education.

A scientist, for example, may leave an academic post to accept a position in the defense hierarchy—in the Advanced Research Projects Agency or in Defense Research and Engineering. Then, after serving for several years, he leaves the Pentagon to take a new job in private industry. Such job hopping by scientists is not uncommon. It certainly does confer an insider's advantage on the company hiring such a defense-wise expert....

Weapons making has obviously escalated into very big business ... [and] has thus taken deep root in postwar American life. But the vast public outlays for weapons have meant constant deferral of projects designed to deal with the human problems of living in crowded cities.

By 1970 this urban neglect had become so acute that the Congress, despite its political involvement in the military-industrial complex, was forced to break out of its bondage. If we invoke the triangular pattern of this military-industrial-political complex, it seems evident that only at its political base was it vulnerable. The military and industrial interests were too great and too self-supportive to permit any attack on these two sides of the triangle.

REPORT ON LOCKHEED AND THE C-5A JET [6]

Air Force Colonel Joe Warren, a crusty cost-efficiency expert, was unmoved by Lockheed Aircraft's attempt to snow him over its C-5A jet transport program. Lockheed's briefing, he wrote air force headquarters . . . [several] years ago, was "like seeing the rerun of an old movie—the plot still has drama and suspense, the script was excellent, the acting superb, but the outcome will be the same as it was the first, second or tenth time it was shown. The contract costs will be exceeded." Warren was right. With the air force refusing to impose tough cost discipline on a favored aerospace contractor, Lockheed has run up one of the most whopping cost overruns ever experienced on a weapons procurement program. Worse still, there's been no change in the inner workings of the military-industrial complex, which precipitated the C-5 disaster.

New evidence I have obtained indicates that at least $1.5 billion of the $2 billion C-5A overrun was clearly avoidable. In the first place, the air force gave Lockheed the contract (probably for the sole reason of keeping the company in business) despite known deficiencies in its design proposal that were sure to lead—and did—to expensive redesign work. Even then, much of the overrun might have been salvaged if the air force had clamped down on excessive plant overhead rates and blatant inefficiency on the production line. But despite the early warnings by Colonel Warren and other cost experts, top air force brass and bureaucrats swept these problems under the rug. At every stage, the air force's primary interest was in concealing the problem, not solving it.

The C-5 program was destined for trouble from the beginning, and here's why: the contract, signed in October 1965, contained a novel provision permitting Lockheed to come in with a low bid to land the program, with the virtual

[6] From "The Lockheed Scandal," by James G. Phillips, former military editor of the *Congressional Quarterly*, author of their 1968 study on defense spending. *New Republic*. 163:19-23. Ag. 1, '70. Reprinted by permission of *The New Republic*, © 1970, Harrison-Blaine of New Jersey, Inc.

assurance of getting bailed out later by the Government in the event of trouble. This provision was called the "repricing formula" by the air force and later the "golden handshake" by critics. It allowed the company to offset at least part of its losses on Production Run A of 58 aircraft by recomputing the price agreed on earlier for Run B of 57 planes. Although the second run would be undertaken at the option of the Government, it appeared almost certain that the air force would want the extra planes and more. Air force long-range airlift plans called for a 120-plane, six-squadron program. The other five planes would be procured from Run C—another option for the purchase of up to 85 planes at a price to be negotiated later.

The "handshake" clause, based on an extremely complicated mathematical formula, provided essentially that if actual costs of Run A exceeded the original contract "target cost" (contract price less profits) by more than 40 per cent, target cost of Run B (set at $490 million in 1965) would be increased by approximately $1.25 for every additional dollar spent on Run A above the 40 per cent cost growth mark. Cost increases of less than 40 per cent would be financed as follows: for increases of 30 per cent or less, Lockheed and the Government would share responsibility, with the Government paying 70 per cent. Lockheed's share would be applied against its projected Run A profits of $128 million, which would be evaporated once costs rose by more than 30 per cent. If the Run B option weren't exercised, Lockheed would bear full responsibility for all cost growth over 30 per cent. But if the air force bought Run B, the "golden handshake" would go into effect once cost growth passed that mark. For cost increases of 30 to 40 per cent, the handshake would reimburse Lockheed 87 cents on every additional dollar it spent, and above 40 per cent, Lockheed would get back $1.25. (Both the 87-cents and $1.25 formulas, however, were pegged to the number of aircraft ordered under Run B, and lesser amounts than these would be paid if the Government bought less than 32 of the Run B planes.)

Once a 40 per cent cost increase appeared likely, the handshake loomed as a reverse incentive encouraging Lockheed to be less efficient. At this point, it would be in the company's interest to run up even greater costs on the initial production run in order to make 25 cents profit on every additional dollar it spent. Because of the sharing formula on the first 40 per cent of extra costs, the cost growth would have to be astronomical before the handshake could turn Run A losses into an overall profit on the program. (The original target profit agreed to for the Run B option was only $49 million.) But at the same time, catastrophic losses would be impossible unless the air force decided not to buy Run B or the company actually lost money on its Run B operation—a prospect that appeared unlikely because aircraft costs per unit characteristically decline as a contractor gains experience with a program. Undoubtedly, this protection against big losses was an important factor in Lockheed's decision to cut corners on its bid.

Desperate for new business, Lockheed's management in early 1965 ordered its staff's lowest cost estimate reduced by 10 per cent in order to undercut its competitors—Douglas Aircraft (now McDonnell-Douglas) and the Boeing Company. Lockheed's bid of $1.9 billion for research and production, including Run B if ordered, was $79 million less than Douglas' and $300 million less than Boeing's. The Lockheed proposal expressed a high degree of technical optimism that was unfounded under the circumstances. It also made little allowance for inflation though the air force had warned all three contractors to take that factor into account as a normal business risk over the first two years of the contract (after that, the contract provided that inflationary increases would be covered largely by the Government). Nor did the Lockheed proposal make allowance for the fact that the C-5 award was the first of a new type of contract called "Total Package Procurement," under which the contractor would commit himself to a fixed price ahead of time for both research and production—a risky proposition that might have given Lockheed pause had it not been for the protection afforded by the golden handshake provision. Although an Air Force Source Selection Board found Boeing's proposal superior in its technical aspects, Lockheed won the contract on the basis of its low cost bid. The entire program was to cost $3.4 billion, including the airframe, engines and spare parts.

In a move to narrow the technical edge held by Boeing, Lockheed had hurriedly adopted certain design changes suggested by the air force just before submitting its bid. It had vastly underpriced the cost of these changes, increasing its bid by only $48 million. At least one high-ranking air force official told company management that its allowance for the changes was far too low, but Lockheed ignored his advice.

Almost from the start of development work in early 1966, air force cost experts assigned to a top-level headquarters management group began citing evidence of a big cost overrun in the making. A. E. Fitzgerald, the deputy for management systems who later was to lose his job after testifying to Congress on the C-5's problems, noted early in the year that overhead rates at the company's production facility in Marietta, Georgia, were vastly exceeding target. Colonel Larry M. Killpack, chief of the air force's Cost and Economic Information Bureau, found by year's end that several key parts of the program were overrun by more than 100 per cent. On December 8, Killpack concluded in a memo to air force headquarters that "Lockheed is in serious difficulty on the C-5A." Five days later, Colonel Warren penned his memo. All these reports fell on deaf ears.

As Lockheed admitted later, the reason for its early overspending was a massive redesign effort related partly to the last-minute technical changes the company had squeezed into its contract proposal. The most significant of these changes had been enlargement of the wing to meet air force requirements for the plane's short-field landing capability. But reconfiguration of the wing brought on weight problems, which required a new round of redesign work. After

Fitzgerald learned of the extent of the redesign effort, he reported that these engineering problems almost certainly would mean a heavy cost impact when the plane moved from research to production.

By late 1966, the C-5's Systems Program Office (SPO), the office charged with day-to-day monitoring of the C-5 contract, joined the efficiency experts in their concern over the C-5's mounting costs. The SPO had become alarmed at indications from Lockheed management that the company did not intend to make good on the full contract performance specifications. One of the developments that bothered the SPO was Lockheed's proposal for a "tradeoff," as the company described it, relaxing the weight requirements in exchange for increased engine thrust, to be provided at Government expense. The proposal was rejected.

In an extraordinary move, the SPO on February 1, 1967, sent Lockheed a "cure notice" indicating the contract would be canceled unless Lockheed presented a satisfactory plan for improvement within the next thirty days. It was the first such action ever taken by the air force on a major weapons program. Although Air Force Headquarters questioned the advisability of the action, the SPO prevailed. Standby press releases announcing the move were prepared both at Wright-Patterson Air Force Base, Ohio, where the SPO is located, and at Air Force Headquarters in Washington. But both were marked for use only in the event of press inquiry, and when press questions failed to develop, neither was ever released. This was one of the most blatant of all the air force's cover-ups and one of the most costly in terms of the public interest. Since the plane had not yet moved into production, disclosure of its problems at this stage might have led to enough pressure to induce the air force to switch the contract to Boeing or at least bear down on costs.

The cure notice evoked tremendous concern at Lockheed, which was then preparing a public offering of $125 million in convertible debentures. Within the next three weeks, Lockheed met repeatedly with the SPO but to no avail. With time running out, Lockheed finally swayed the SPO on February 21, by promising to dispatch a top-level technical team from corporate headquarters in California to help the foundering Lockheed-Georgia management resolve the plane's technical problems. The cure notice was rescinded.

Despite the presence of the headquarters technical team, it was business as usual on the production line. Colonel Jack W. Tooley, a former army airlift expert working as a civilian adviser to Lockheed, reported that he observed incredible inefficiency in the plant. "From time to time," he recalled recently, "since I had nothing better to do, I would walk through the main plant, observing what was going on. The number of workers loafing on the job was absolutely unbelievable. . . .

The situation was not much better at General Electric's plant in Evendale, Ohio, where the C-5's engines were under production. Here Fitzgerald also found excessive overhead rates and a large part of the work force loafing. After one trip to the facility in early 1967, Fitzgerald wrote air force headquarters: "I observed a total of 134 people, of whom 35, or 26 per cent, appeared to be working. The modal pace of work was quite low, approximately 70 per cent of normal. Machine utilization appeared to be about 50 per cent on the day shift and lower still on the swing shift." Fitzgerald later told Congress that at least $1 billion of the C-5 overrun could have been saved if the air force had required reasonable efficiency and economy of work forces at the Lockheed and GE plants.

Annoyed by the continuous appearance of cost analysts, Lockheed and their sympathizers in the Pentagon began seeking their systematic exclusion from the program. Orders were cut sending Warren to Addis Ababa as air attaché. Fitzgerald and other friends of Warren at air force headquarters were able to block that appointment, but Warren was still removed from the program and assigned to a Pentagon computer manager job. Killpack was transferred to Vietnam, and Tooley quit Lockheed-Georgia in disgust.

With its technical problems mounting, Lockheed turned to costly and exotic materials such as titanium to help pare down the excess weight. By now the company had found it was useless to try to wiggle out of contract specifications. Despite some expressions of unhappiness at higher levels, the SPO refused to budge.

Without doubt, the SPO's adherence to the contract dealt Lockheed a stunning blow. When the company had run into production problems on earlier programs, the air force would often waive specifications or provide enough contract change orders (sometimes called "contract nourishment" in the trade) to ensure that the company came out well. Lockheed's chief development engineer on the program later told Securities and Exchange Commission investigators that he never suspected the C-5 contract would be enforced. . . . In its 1969 report to stockholders, the company said the air force's strict insistence on performance specifications and delivery dates "resulted in expenses by contractor far beyond the original estimate to avoid ever-present threats of cancellation for default. . . . Contract terms were regarded as sacrosanct even though a relaxation of specifications and delivery dates could have greatly lessened costs."

In May 1967, Lockheed moved from research to the production phase of the program with the plane's technical problems far from resolved. At a meeting of the top-level air force management group, at least one official complained that more time should have been spent on development. "This is the first major aircraft system," he said, "to begin operational systems development after completing an extensive contract definition phase. The central idea of contract definition is to define achievable performance and to develop realistic schedules and credible cost estimates in relation thereto. Clearly, Lockheed flunks the course on this basis."

Despite continuing SPO concern over the technical difficulties, Lockheed characterized the problems as nonrecurring and refused to acknowledge their potential impact on costs. Late in 1967, Lockheed-Georgia notified corporate headquarters that "the bulk of the program remains before us, giving us ample opportunity for cost savings. . . ." Although Lockheed added a $90 million contingency fund to its cost estimates by the end of 1967, it explained to its auditor, Arthur Young Company, that it was merely being conservative and that the funds would not be needed. Arthur Young's notes indicate unbounded optimism on Lockheed's part. The first indication of a really disastrous overrun on the Lockheed program came in April 1968, when the SPO estimated costs of $2.9 billion through Run B, a $1 billion overrun. The SPO figured Lockheed had known about the cost situation since the early part of the year, since the company at that time . . . "intensified their efforts to maneuver within the contract framework to get the air force to pay for work we contend is already on contract. In addition, they started attempting to limit our visibility on program costs.". . .

But with a decision soon due on the Run B option, Lockheed decided to adopt a low profile and hope that, as before, air force headquarters would not become unduly alarmed at another pessimistic SPO estimate. As the SEC [Securities and Exchange Commission] staff put it, the rebuttal package was ready if needed "to help protect Lockheed's position in this respect, but would not be used unless necessary because of the danger of focusing attention on the cost increase." The SPO apparently recognized this same motive in June when it wrote that it was definitely in Lockheed's favor to keep the air force "in the dark" on the costs of Run A, because of their potentially adverse impact on a decision to exercise the Run B option.

At this point, however, even the SPO, which had been relatively tough on Lockheed, became concerned over the effect that disclosure of its cost projections might have on the company's liquidity position. Its reports to higher headquarters contained the following notation: "Security considerations. You will see we are estimating that Lockheed will overrun the ceiling price of the contract by a significant margin, that is, they will incur large monetary losses on the program. The SPO has treated this information as extremely sensitive in view of the adverse publicity and stock market implications." SPO said there was no pressure from Lockheed or higher headquarters to insert this warning in its report. It said the suggestion was made "purely and simply because the cost figures . . . were estimates and were not concurred in by the contractor. There was a wide variation between the estimate contained in this report and the contractor's estimate. It was felt that should the air force prove to be inaccurate subsequent to wide public disclosure, the air force would be accused of acting irresponsibly."

Instead, the SPO decided to err on the side of the contractor and let the public be damned. Air force headquarters moved quickly to close off possible leaks by directing that the information be limited to top-level reports and be excluded from any document receiving wide circulation. Although Congress had been notified of the SPO's August 1967 estimate of a $331 million overrun, it was not informed of the new projection. Neither was it told of a follow-up study in October, which placed the overrun on the entire program at $2 billion, including $1.5 billion on the Lockheed program. The SEC staff revealed that the air force considered rewriting performance specifications at this point to give Lockheed a better break. (Some of the performance specifications were relaxed later, and the air force now is planning significant further relaxation in order to avoid another costly redesign of the wing.)

The next episode came in early November, when Richard Kaufman, staff economist for the joint Congressional Economic Committee's Economy in Government Subcommittee, was setting up a subcommittee hearing on "The Economics of Military Procurement." Kaufman had followed the C-5 program closely and knew of the latest overrun estimate. Although no subcommittee member or staffer had yet contacted Fitzgerald, several Pentagon associates recommended him.

When Kaufman invited Fitzgerald to testify, bedlam broke loose in the Pentagon. Defense Department Comptroller Robert Moot, the Pentagon's top financial officer, warned Fitzgerald that his testimony "would leave blood on the floor." The Pentagon sought to substitute a more manageable witness, but the subcommittee chairman, Senator William Proxmire (Democrat, Wisconsin), insisted that Fitzgerald appear. Finally, the Pentagon agreed to let Fitzgerald attend as a backup witness. At the hearing November 13, Proxmire ignored the Pentagon's hand-picked witness and called Fitzgerald immediately to the stand. Fitzgerald confirmed Proxmire's estimate of the $2 billion overrun, leading to his immediate removal from the program and eventual dismissal from his job.

With Congress and the public enraged about the overrun, the Pentagon flatly repudiated Proxmire's figures. Its Public Affairs Office put out a release contending that current estimates for the program were only $4.3 billion instead of the $5.3 billion Proxmire had revealed. Supplementary material requested of Fitzgerald for the hearing record was altered by the Pentagon to show the lower figure. The difference turned out to be the air force's omission of some $900 million for spare parts—another item that was badly overrun. The spares were mostly engines and ground equipment—items the air force classifies as an operating cost and not as original investment. The Pentagon news release failed to make this distinction, however, thus conveying the impression that Proxmire was overstating costs.

Despite opposition from the Defense Department's Systems Analysis Office, which sought to limit the C-5 program to three squadrons, the air force on January 14, 1969, exercised the Run B option, but instructed Lockheed for the time being to limit production to long-leadtime items for only twenty-three more planes. On grounds of budgetary restraints, the air force announced last October [1969] that it would curtail the program after completion of eighty-one planes. With the effect of the golden handshake formula now blunted (because the air force was ordering less than ninety planes), Lockheed stood to lose more than $500 million. Contending the Pentagon's exercise of the Run B option required purchase of all fifty-seven Run B planes, Lockheed sued the Government for default. (Lockheed now figures it would have broken even on the full 115-plane program.)

The cozy relationships of this military-industrial complex came to light again this spring when Lockheed requested $640 million in emergency financing and Pentagon officials, backed by military enthusiasts in Congress, sought to expedite the company's claim. Even when the Pentagon learned that Lockheed's immediate cash problem had resulted from its commercial program—the L-1011 "airbus" —it still maintained its support of the proposed bailout money. Lockheed was a national asset like the redwood tree.

Even the Securities and Exchange Commission (but not its tough-minded staff) has shown sympathy for the embattled contractor. At the completion of the SEC staff's year-long investigation of Lockheed's cost disclosures on the C-5 program and alleged illegal dumping of company stock by corporate insiders, the Commission announced June 2 that the investigation "did not disclose evidence of unlawful insider trading." The Commission's terse announcement seemed at odds with the findings of the staff's report. Citing specific instances of heavy selling by top corporate officers at critical junctures in the program, the staff raised the "possibility that this was done on the basis of inside information." Rumors abounded that the staff had recommended indictments; the SEC denied it.

Although the SEC release announced the Commission's decision to study cost disclosures on a number of weapon contracts, including the C-5A, it gave no indication of the staff's considerable misgivings over Lockheed's disclosure policy on the C-5 program. In its report, the staff raised the question of "the adequacy of disclosure in annual and interim filings with the Commission and with the [New York Stock] Exchange as well as information prepared for public distribution." The staff also raised questions as to the adequacy of Lockheed's description of the cure notice in a registration statement it filed with the SEC in March 1967, covering the $125 million debenture issue. The Commission at first put the staff report under wraps but later made it public under stiff pressure from Congress.

As I said earlier, much of the C-5 overrun could have been avoided if the air force had really cracked down. Of the $2 billion overrun, less than $200 million can be attributed to inflation. The rest is due entirely to Lockheed's redesign effort and pure inefficiency on the Lockheed and GE production lines. Even if Lockheed had charged an extra $200-$250 million in the beginning to get its design up to a par with Boeing's (or by that same token if the contract had gone to Boeing), the whole program should have cost no more than $3.8 billion, given reasonable efficiency. Thus about $1.5 billion of the overrun should have been saved. As it is, the air force estimates that even the eighty-one-plane program is going to cost $4.6 billion—$1.2 billion more than the original contract estimate for 115 planes. Thus far, the air force has spent $2.5 billion on the program and has received one operable plane!

[On February 1, 1971, Lockheed accepted, after initially rejecting, a Pentagon offer to pay out all of some $758 million of disputed costs for the C-5A provided Lockheed paid back $200 million of this over a period of years as a "fixed loss." By that time Lockheed had been paid $3.827 billion under the original contract, some thirty of the planes had been delivered, and the estimated cost of the 81 planes to be delivered by 1973 according to the curtailed contract had risen to $4.585 billion, or about $56 million per plane. It was unofficially estimated that the total cost of 115 C-5As, as called for in the original contract, would be well in excess of $6 billion.—Ed.]

THE EVOLUTION OF
THE NEW STATE-MANAGEMENT [7]

In the name of defense, and without announcement or debate, a basic alteration has been effected in the governing institutions of the United States. An industrial management has been installed in the Federal Government, under the Secretary of Defense, to control the nation's largest network of industrial enterprises. With the characteristic managerial propensity for extending its power, limited only by its allocated share of the national product, the new state-management combines peak economic, political, and military decision making. Hitherto, this combination of powers in the same hands has been a feature of statist societies—Communist, Fascist, and others—where individual rights cannot constrain central rule.

This new institution of state-managerial control has been the result of actions undertaken for the declared purposes of adding to military power and economic efficiency and of reinforcing civilian, rather than, professional, military rule. Its main characteristics are institutionally specific and therefore substantially independent of its chief of the moment. The effects of its operations are independent of the intention of its architects, and may even have been unforeseen by them.

The creation of the state-management marked the transformation of President Dwight Eisenhower's "military-industrial complex," a loose collaboration, mainly through market relations, of senior military officers, industrial managers, and legislators. Robert McNamara, under the direction of President John Kennedy, organized a formal central-management office to administer the military-industrial empire. The market was replaced by a management. In place of the complex, there is now a defined administrative control center that regulates tens of thousands of subordinate managers.

[7] From *Pentagon Capitalism: The Political Economy of War*, by Seymour Melman, professor of industrial engineering, Columbia University. McGraw. '70. p 1-7. Copyright © 1970 by Seymour Melman. Used with permission of McGraw-Hill Book Company.

In 1968, they directed the production of $44 billion of goods and services for military use. By the measure of the scope and scale of its decision-power, the new state-management is by far the largest and most important single management in the United States. There are about 15,000 men who arrange work assignments to subordinate managers (contract negotiation), and 40,000 who oversee compliance of submanagers of subdivisions with the top management's rules. This is the largest industrial central administrative office in the United States—perhaps in the world.

The state-management has also become the most powerful decision-making unit in the United States Government. Thereby, the Federal Government does not "serve" business or "regulate" business. For the new management is the largest of them all. Government *is* business. That is state capitalism.

The normal operation, including expansion, of the new state-management has been based upon preemption of a lion's share of Federal tax revenue and of the nation's finite supply of technical manpower. This use of capital and skill has produced parasitic economic growth—military products which are not part of the level of living and which cannot be used for further production. All this, while the ability to defend the United States, to shield it from external attack, has diminished.

From 1946 to 1969, the United States Government spent over $1,000 billion on the Military, more than half of this under the Kennedy and Johnson Administrations—the period during which the state-management was established as a formal institution. This sum of staggering size (try to visualize a billion of something) does not express the cost of the Military Establishment to the nation as a whole. The true cost is measured by what has been forgone, by the accumulated deterioration in many facets of life, by the inability to alleviate human wretchedness of long duration.

Here is part of the human inventory of depletion:

1. By 1968, there were 6 million grossly substandard dwell-ings, mainly in the cities.
2. 10 million Americans suffered from hunger in 1968-1969.
3. The United States ranked eighteenth at last report (1966) among nations in infant mortality rate (23.7 infant deaths in first year per 1,000 live births). In Sweden (1966) the rate was 12.6.
4. In 1967, 40.7 per cent of the young men examined were disqualified for military service (28.5 per cent for medi-cal reasons).
5. In 1950, there were 109 physicians in the United States per 100,000 population. By 1966 there were 98.
6. About 30 million Americans are an economically under-developed sector of the society.

The human cost of military priority is paralleled by the industrial-technological depletion caused by the concentra-tion of technical manpower and capital on military tech-nology and in military industry. For example:

1. By 1968, United States industry operated the world's oldest stock of metal-working machinery; 64 per cent was 10 years old and over.
2. No United States railroad has anything in motion that compares with the Japanese and French fast trains.
3. The United States merchant fleet ranks 23rd in age of vessels. In 1966, world average-age of vessels was 17 years, United States 21, Japan 9.
4. While the United States uses the largest number of re-search scientists and engineers in the world, key United States industries, such as steel and machine tools, are in trouble in domestic markets: in 1967, for the first time, the United States imported more machine tools than it exported.

As civilian industrial technology deteriorates or fails to ad-vance, productive employment opportunity for Americans diminishes.

All of this only begins to reckon the true cost to America of operating the state military machine. (The cost of the Vietnam war to the Vietnamese people has no reckoning.) Clearly, no mere ideology or desire for individual power can account for the colossal costs of the military machine. A lust for power has been at work here, but it is not explicable in terms of an individual's power drive. Rather, the state-management represents an institutionalized power-lust. A normal thirst for more managerial power within the largest management in the United States gives the new state-management an unprecedented ability and opportunity for building a military-industry empire at home and for using this as an instrument for building an empire abroad. This is the new imperialism.

The magnitude of the decision-power of the Pentagon management has reached that of a state. After all, the fiscal 1970 budget plan of the Department of Defense—*$83 billion* —exceeds the gross national product (GNP) of entire nations: in billions of dollars for 1966—Belgium, $18.1; Italy $61.4; Sweden $21.3. The state-management has become a parastate, a state within a state.

In its beginning, the Government of the United States was a political entity. The managing of economic and industrial activity was to be the province of private persons. This division of function was the grand design for American Government and society, within which personal and political freedom could flourish alongside of rapid economic growth and technological progress. After 1960, this design was transformed. In the name of ensuring civilian control over the Department of Defense and of obtaining efficiencies of modern management, Secretary of Defense Robert McNamara redesigned the organization of his department to include, within the office of the Secretary, a central administrative office. This was designed to control operations in thousands of subsidiary industrial enterprises undertaken on behalf of the Department of Defense. Modeled after the central administrative offices of multidivision industrial firms—such as the Ford Motor Company, the General Motors Corporation, and the General Electric Company—the new top management in the Department of Defense was designed to control the activities of subsidiary managements of firms producing, in 1968, $44 billion of goods and services for the Department of Defense.

By the measure of industrial activity governed from one central office, this new management in the Department of Defense is beyond compare the largest industrial management in the United States, perhaps in the world. Never before in American experience has there been such a combination of economic and political decision-power in the same hands. The senior officers of the new state-management are also senior political officers of the Government of the United States. Thus, one consequence of the establishment of the new state-management has been the installation, within American society, of an institutional feature of a totalitarian system.

The original design of the American Government was oriented toward safeguarding individual political freedom and economic liberties. These safeguards were abridged by the establishment of the new state-management in the Department of Defense. In order to perceive the abridgment of traditional liberties by the operation of the new managerial institution, one must focus on its functional performance. For the official titles of its units sound like just another Government bureaucracy: Office of the Secretary of Defense, Defense Supply Agency, etc.

The new industrial management has been created in the name of defending America from its external enemies and preserving a way of life of a free society. It has long been understood, however, that one of the safeguards of individual liberty is the separation of roles of a citizen and of an employee. When an individual relates to the same person both as a citizen and as an employee, then the effect is such—regardless of intention—that the employer-government official has an unprecedented combination of decision-making power over the individual citizen-employee.

In the Soviet Union, the combination of top economic and political decision-power is a formal part of the organization and ideology of that society. In the United States, in contrast, the joining of the economic-managerial and top political power has been done in an unannounced and, in effect, covert fashion. In addition to the significance of the new state-management with respect to individual liberty in American society, the new organization is significant for its effects in preempting resources and committing the nation to the military operations that the new organization is designed to serve. Finally, the new power center is important because of the self-powered drive toward expansion that is built into the normal operation of an industrial management.

The preemption of resources takes place because of the sheer size of the funds that are wielded by the Department of Defense. Its budget, amounting to over $80 billion in 1969, gives this organization and its industrial-management arm unequaled decision-power over manpower, materials, and industrial production capacity in the United States and abroad. It is, therefore, predictable that this organization will be able to get the people and other resources that it needs whenever it needs them, even if this requires outbidding other industries and other organizations—including other agencies of the Federal and other governments.

Regardless of the individual avowals and commitments of the principal officers of the new industrial machine, it is necessarily the case that the increased competence of this organization contributes to the competence of the parent body—the Department of Defense. This competence is a war-making capability. Hence, the very efficiency and success of the new industrial-management, unavoidably and regardless of intention, enhances the war-making capability of the Government of the United States. As the war-making department accumulates diverse resources and planning capability, it is able to offer the President blueprint-stage options for responding to all manner of problem situations —while other Government agencies look (and are) unready, understaffed, and underequipped. This increases the likelihood of recourse to "solutions" based upon military power.

Finally, the new Government management, insofar as it shares the usual characteristics of industrial management, has a built-in propensity for expanding the scope and intensity of its operations—for this expansion is the hallmark of success in management. The chiefs of the new state-management, in order to be successful in their own eyes, strive to maintain and extend their decision-power—by enlarging their activities, the number of their employees, the size of the capital investments which they control, and by gaining control over more and more subsidiary managements. By 1967-1968, the scope of the state-management's control over production had established it as the dominant decision-maker in U.S. industry. The industrial output of $44 billion of goods and services under state-management control in 1968 exceeded by far the reported net sales of American industry's leading firms (in billions of dollars for 1968): AT&T [American Telephone & Telegraph Company], $14.1; du Pont, $3.4; General Electric $8.4; General Motors, $2.8; United States Steel, $4.6. The giants of United States industry have become small- and medium-sized firms, compared with the new state-management—with its conglomerate industrial base.

The appearance of the new state-managerial machine marks a transformation in the character of the American Government and requires us to reexamine our understanding of its behavior. Various classic theories of industrial capitalist society have described government as an essentially political entity, ideally impartial. Other theories depict government as justifiably favoring, or even identifying with, business management, while the theories in the Marxist tradition have depicted government as an arm of business. These theories require revision.

THE STATE WITHIN A STATE: AN ESSAY ON
PENTAGON CAPITALISM [8]

The thesis of Seymour Melman's terrifying book [*Pentagon Capitalism: The Political Economy of War*] can be briefly stated. There exists within the democratic capitalist political economy of the United States a second political economy that is neither capitalist nor democratic. Technically subordinate to the larger entity, this second political economy has in fact become the acknowledged master of the industrial core of the primary economic system, and the silent master of crucial areas of its political life. Each year the directorship of this inner state, through appeals of mixed fear and patriotism, renews its control over the richest portion to its industrial satrapies.

In the process of rewarding its vassals, the central management casts an indulgent eye on the excesses of its supporters, and takes care to shore up weaker members lest by their disappearance the boundaries of the inner state shrink. Finally, and most important, the state within a state has a double significance for the society in which it is entrenched. Presumptively the inner state serves as a mighty striking force whose purpose is to make invincible the nation's will. In fact, however, the inner state is the Achilles' heel of the outer, not only robbing it of energies and creativity that cannot be pried loose from the insatiable demands of the military, but threatening by its very presence to invite the total destruction that even its immense striking force cannot prevent.

So much for rhetoric. Now a few facts. The system of military production and distribution managed by the Department of Defense (DOD) is the largest planned economy outside the Soviet Union. Its property—plant and equipment, land and inventories of war commodities—amounts to some $202 billion, or about 10 per cent of the assets of the

[8] From "Military America," by Robert L. Heilbroner, author and economist. *New York Review of Books.* 15:5. Jl. 23, '70. Reprinted with permission from *The New York Review of Books.* Copyright © 1970 Robert Heilbroner.

entire American economy. It owns 39 million acres of land; rules a population of 4.7 million direct employees or soldiers; and spends over $80 billion a year. This makes it richer than any small nation in the world, and of course incomparably more powerful. That part of its assets which is represented by nuclear explosives alone gives the DOD the equivalent of six tons of TNT for every inhabitant on the globe, to which must be added a "conventional" military capability of gargantuan proportions: the explosives dropped on South and North Vietnam so far amount to 3 million tons, or 50 per cent more than the total bomb tonnage dropped in both the European and Pacific theatres during World War II.

The DOD system embraces both men and industry. The men include, first, 3.5 million soldiers deployed in 2,257 bases or locations abroad and in numerous camps at home and 1.2 million civilian employees located both at home and abroad. No less important is an industrial army of at least 3 million workers who are directly employed on war production, in addition to a considerably larger number employed as the secondary echelon of "defense-related" production. This does not include still further millions who owe their livelihood to the civilian services they render to the military workers themselves. I would guess that if the DOD simply shut down tomorrow and nothing took its place, unemployment would probably rise from its present 5 per cent of the labor force to over 15 per cent, roughly as in 1931. But of course the DOD will not shut down. Hence a more significant index of its extent of command over manpower may be that 63 per cent of all U.S. scientists, engineers, and technicians work on defense projects of one kind or another.

Pentagon control over industry stems from the immense flow of DOD expenditure. Merely by way of indicating its size we might note that a peripheral activity, the Post Exchange (PX) system, is the third largest distribution network in the country (just after Sears and the A&P) and that the construction of housing facilities for the military cost more, from 1965 to 1967, than the total spent by the Federal Government on all other public housing. At the core, however, lies the real source of DOD control—a stream of forty-odd billion dollars of production contracts for the renewal and expansion of its actual military equipment.

This flow of expenditure comprises the main source of income for a small number of highly specialized industrial enterprises that are in fact nothing but Government arsenals spun off as "private enterprises," and a substantial source of income for a much larger number. One expects Lockheed (88 per cent of sales to the Government) to figure as a major benefactor; one does not expect Pan Am (44 per cent of sales . . . 1960-67). Altogether it is estimated that between 15,000 and 20,000 firms are prime contractors with the DOD, but since almost all prime contractors subcontract (and since subcontractors also subcontract), the number who ultimately benefit may be three times as large.

Within this large constituency, a relatively small number of firms are the main recipients of DOD awards. The hundred largest defense contractors supplied two thirds of the forty-odd billion dollars of deliveries (although they in turn actively subcontracted their own large contracts); and within this group an *inner* inner core of ten firms (McDonnell-Douglas, General Dynamics, Lockheed, General Electric, United Aircraft, Boeing, North American, AT&T, General Motors, and Ling-Temco-Vought) all by themselves accounted for 30 per cent of the total. Incidentally, many of the largest contractors not only owe their sales volume to the DOD, but a considerable fraction of their capital; as of 1967, defense contractors used $2 billion worth of Government-owned furniture and office machines, $4.7 billion worth of materials, and over $5 billion worth of plant and equipment, on all of which, of course, they were allowed to make profits just as if they were using their own property.

Note: "allowed" to make profits. For as Melman emphasizes, at the heart of the Pentagon system lies a crucial struc-

ture of centralized management through which the economic activities of the industrial empire are shaped according to the wishes of the Pentagon officialdom. To run the
military business of the United States takes some 15 million
purchasing decisions per year, and a vastly larger number
of administrative decisions. Responsibility for this gigantic
activity rests with a DOD bureaucracy of 15,000 individuals
empowered to arrange terms of contract at various levels of
importance, in addition to another 25,000 who administer,
oversee, check, and carry out the contractual arrangements.

These arrangements give the DOD virtual life-and-death
powers over its industrial suppliers, permitting the prepay-
ment of hundreds of millions of dollars, on the one hand,
or the dire penalty of contract cancellation, on the other.
These powers are exercised according to codified regulations
published by the DOD but capable, as are all such regulations, of infinite interpretation when circumstances demand.
Thus "efficiency," which is a prime requirement of suppliers,
can be stretched to permit the award of the rich F-111 contract to General Dynamics, despite its poorer performance
and higher bid than Boeing, and "honesty" can be taken to
include the submission of some $10 billion of questionable
charges annually (according to an estimate based on a study
of a sample of contractors six years ago).

All this merely indicates that the smile of the DOD is
all-important for suppliers, who then report the results to
their stockholders as "profit." The same fiction of "free private enterprise" is maintained when things turn out less well,
and a project is finally canceled (between 1953 and 1968,
sixty-eight projects were terminated, although not before
$10.5 billion had been expended on them). In that case the
resulting penalty for the contracting firm is called a "loss."

Supervising and directing this entire system is the topmost echelon of the parastate—a group of career generals,
professional Government administrators, professorial advisers, and former businessmen, culminating in the offices
of the President and the Secretary of Defense and the Joint

Chiefs of Staff, powerfully supported by a few people within the House of Representatives and the Senate. It is these individuals who ultimately guide the striking force itself, turning it against the Dominican Republic or Vietnam, or simply authorizing its further growth as part of the system of "deterrence" by which the two great powers maintain their uneasy truce.

This topmost group is guided in its decisions by a view of the world in which our own activities are uniformly interpreted as actions in the service of peace and humanity, and in which the activities of the other side are uniformly interpreted as actual or potential moves of aggression and threats to human well-being. This ideological justification for the maintenance of our Military Establishment thus provides the rationale for the continuous search for, and discovery of, weaknesses in our armed posture, as the DOD unearths missile gaps, bomber gaps, antiballistic missile gaps, etc., each of which thereupon provides a further reason for the expansion and strengthening of the military inner state.

Last, but by no means least, there is the question of what constituency the military system serves—who stands behind its actions, both political and economic? Professor Melman gives us the following list:

> The administrative staff of the state-management [of the DOD]
> Career men, military and civilian, in the armed forces
> People working in military industry
> People working in the military research-and-development establishment
> Communities and parts of communities dependent on military industries and bases
> Many members of Congress representing areas of high military activity
> Believers in a world Communist conspiracy against the United States
> People of strongly authoritarian personalities, who identify with martial leadership

There are, of course, also groups that are opposed to the state-military machine, groups, one hopes, whose strength will increase as the machine demonstrates its futility in Vietnam and its parasitic absorption of energies at home. But it is clear that up to the present, at least, the forces supporting the system are stronger than those opposing—that the parastate is essentially a trusted and popular rather than an unwelcome and feared institution. From this there follows an interlocking of the stimuli of fear and the response of renewed support that makes the system a closed loop, continuously reinforcing its power and position within American society.

"Rarely does a single social force have a controlling influence in changing, swiftly, the character of life in a large and complex society," Melman concludes. "The expansion of the Pentagon and its state-management is such a force. Failing decisive action to reverse the economic and other growth of these institutions, then the parent state, if it is saved from nuclear war, will surely become the guardian of a garrison-like society dominated by the Pentagon and its state-management." . . .

Is the Military Establishment—the state within a state—in fact independent of its economic and political host? The issue is of surpassing importance, but I confess myself unable to determine how it is to be answered before history answers it for us. In a subdued way, our present situation seems to resemble the ambiguous relation between the chieftains Big Business and the Fascist movements in Italy and Germany—relationships in which business at first welcomed but then lived to regret Fascist power, which took over in its own right.

Up to the time of the Vietnam war there seems to have been a general congruence between the aims of the Military Establishment and those of the business community, since the expansion of the former meant the prosperity of the latter. Only recently have misgivings begun to surface, with the realization that the expansionism of the military parastate has meant—over and beyond the disaster of the war itself—a climate of inflation, preempted talents, and social neglect that has been bad for the general run of business. What we have, now, is a growing division within the ranks of the business community, as between those whose interests are tied to the military sector and those whose interests are beginning to be threatened by it.

In the coming few years this conflict must be resolved in one way or another. I would agree with Melman that capitalism, as a socioeconomic order founded on private property, is not inherently warlike, as witness Sweden, Switzerland, or Canada, and that the system is capable of considerable social flexibility and strength, as the same countries will also illustrate. I would also agree that there exists today in America the nucleus of a garrison state which, while using the institutions of capitalism, is ultimately moved by its own conception of world affairs.

In the disillusions of the Vietnam war, the growth of that garrison state has now been checked. But I suspect that the question whether there will be a peaceful capitalism or a resumption of the hegemony of military state-capitalism will not be finally resolved until the Vietnam war at last peters out and the American economy is faced with the challenge of converting to a peacetime basis.

That huge and potentially life-saving transformation will require national planning on a vast scale, for which we have made no preparations, and before the prospect of which our latent conservatism may rise up to impose insuperable obstacles. In that event, our economy will falter, and the appeal of a return to the arms of the DOD [Department of Defense] will be very great. I do not know how to estimate the chances of our successful economic reorientation. I can only say that if we fail, the general prospect outlined by Seymour Melman seems the most likely course for the American nation to take, an eventuality that should make all men despair.

EDITOR'S INTRODUCTION

In this section are presented samples of the published views of supporters of the Defense Establishment as presently constituted. The opening excerpt is from a Senate speech by Barry Goldwater in reply to the speech by Senator Proxmire which is excerpted at the opening of Section II. This is followed by excerpts from a speech by an Arizona representative, from one by the president of one of the largest defense industries (he is also replying to Senator Proxmire), and from one by Ira C. Eaker, a famous air force general in World War II. Then come excerpts from a highly significant interview with the chairman (in 1970) of the Joint Chiefs of Staff, a selection from a book by another famous air force general who also served as chairman of the Joint Chiefs, and, finally, a criticism of a proposed reorganization of the Defense Department written by the executive vice president of the Southern States Industrial Council.

Attackers and defenders of the structure start from widely different premises and shape their arguments within wholly different systems of value. Critics of the Defense Department and the armaments industry, as a rule, are convinced that the Communist menace is greatly exaggerated, but beyond that they do not address themselves to the question of our relative strength vis-à-vis Russia and Red China. As shown in Section II, they concentrate instead on the economic, social, and political costs of the armaments establishment. The defenders of the structure, represented in this section, minimize such matters and point up benefits carried over into civilian life from technological breakthroughs. Their overriding concern, however, is defense of the country against an implacable foe bent on world domination and determined to use any and all means to achieve it. They insist that the only deterrent to Communist ambition is our armed strength and that therefore there is an overwhelming need for military power. They then proceed to analyses of Communist strength relative to our own, of possible or probable Communist moves, and of the countermoves we must make.

Perhaps what is needed to resolve the basic issues is the kind of holistic thinking which Donald Nelson is described as doing in "The Ordeal of Donald Nelson" in Section I, and which President Eisenhower called for in his Farewell Address (see "A Presidential Warning," also in Section I).

A REPLY TO CRITICISM OF THE DEFENSE ESTABLISHMENT [1]

Judging from the view expressed by many of our public officials and commentators the so-called military-industrial complex would seem to be responsible for almost all of the world's evils. . . .

Let us take the military-industrial complex and examine it closely. What it amounts to is that we have a big Military Establishment, and we have a big industrial plant which helps to supply that establishment. This apparently constitutes a complex. If so, I certainly can find nothing to criticize but much to be thankful for in its existence.

Ask yourselves, for example, why we have a large, expensive Military Establishment and why we have a large and capable defense industry. The answer is simply this: We have huge worldwide responsibilities. We face tremendous worldwide challenges. In short, we urgently require both a big Defense Establishment and a big industrial capacity. Both are essential to our safety and to the preservation of freedom in a world fraught with totalitarian aggression.

[1] From "The Military-Industrial Complex," a speech before the United States Senate, April 15, 1969, by Barry Goldwater (Republican, Arizona). Congressional Record. 115 (daily):9127-9. Ap. 15, '69.

Merely because our huge responsibilities necessitate the existence of a military-industrial complex does not automatically make that complex something we must fear or feel ashamed of....

What would the critics of the military-industrial complex have us do? Would they have us ignore the fact that progress occurs in the field of national defense as well as in the field of social sciences? Do they want us to turn back the clock, disband our Military Establishment, and do away with our defense-related industrial capacity?

Mr. President, do these critics of what they term a military-industrial complex really want us to default on our worldwide responsibilities, turn our back on aggression and slavery, and develop a national policy of selfish isolation?

Rather than deploring the existence of a military-industrial complex, I say we should thank heavens for it. That complex gives us our protective shield. It is the bubble under which our nation thrives and prospers. It is the armor which is unfortunately required in a world divided.

For all those who complain about the military-industrial complex, I ask this question: "What would you replace it with? Would you have the Government do it?" Well, our Government has tried it in the past, and failed—dismally so.

What is more, I believe it is fair to inquire whether the name presently applied is inclusive enough. Consider the large number of scientists who contributed all of the fundamental research necessary to develop and build nuclear weapons and other products of today's defense industries. Viewing this, should not we call it the "scientific-military-industrial complex?"

By the same token, do not forget the amount of research that has gone on in our colleges and universities in support of our defense-related projects. Maybe we should call it an "educational-scientific-military-industrial complex." Then, of course, the vast financing that goes into this effort certainly makes the economic community an integral part of any such complex. Now we have a name that runs like this: "An economic-educational-scientific-military-industrial complex."

What we are talking about, Mr. President, is an undertaking which grew up from necessity. It is the product of American initiative, incentive, and genius responding to a huge global challenge. It is, perhaps, the most effective and efficient complex ever built to fill a worldwide function. Its ultimate aim is peace in our time, regardless of the aggressive, militaristic image which the left wing is attempting to give it.

Mr. President, I do not find the employment of military officers by one hundred of the largest companies in this nation alarming or menacing. Many of those officers were technically trained to provide special services, many of which are required by the companies involved. And I hasten to point out that these same companies employ other free Americans, some of them former senators, some of them former congressmen, some of them former civilian employees of the Government.

It is my contention that a retired military officer is a private citizen. He has a right to seek employment wherever he can. It is only natural that he should look to sources of employment which involve matters he was trained to work in. The fact that he once was an army officer and the company he works for does business with the army does not automatically insure an undesirable relationship from the public viewpoint. . . .

As I have pointed out, many of the problems that are being encountered in the area of national defense today stem not so much from a military-industrial complex as they do from the mistakes and miscalculations of a "civilian complex" or perhaps I should say a "civilian-computer-complex." My reference here, of course, is to the Pentagon hierarchy of young civilians—often referred to as the "whiz kids"

—which was erected during the McNamara era in the questionable name of "cost effectiveness." And this complex, Mr. President, was built in some measure to shut out the military voice in a large area of defense policy decision making.

I suggest that the military-industrial complex is not the all-powerful structure that our liberal friends would have us believe. Certainly nobody can deny that this combination took a drubbing at the hands of Mr. McNamara and his civilian cadres during the past eight years.

If the military-industrial complex had been as strong and as cohesive as its critics would have us believe, it is entirely possible this nation and its taxpayers would not today be facing the need for rebuilding the defenses of freedom. . . .

If the military-industrial complex had been the irresistible giant its critics describe, we would certainly today be better equipped. We would undoubtedly have a nuclear-powered navy adequate to the challenge presented by the Soviet naval might. We would certainly have in the air—and not just on a drawing board—a manned, carry-on bomber. We would never have encountered the kind of shortages which cropped up in every area of the military as a result of the demands from Vietnam. There would have been no shortage of military helicopters. There would have been no shortage of trained helicopter pilots. There would have been no need to use outdated and faulty equipment. No concern ever would have arisen over whether our supply of bombs was sufficient to the task in Southeast Asia. . . .

I have great faith in the civilian leaders of our Government and of our military services. I have no desire to see the voice of the military become all-powerful or even dominant in our national affairs. But I do believe that the military viewpoint must always be heard in the highest councils of our Government in all matters directly affecting the protection and security of our nation.

INSTANT MYTHS ABOUT DEFENSE PROGRAMS [2]

In our few minutes together today, I want to share with you some thoughts on four aspects of people's thinking about defense programs.

First, let's talk about what people believe as to future threats to our country. As I move around among members of Congress and around the United States more broadly, people seem to be using two quite different crystal balls, and these two crystal balls show them two very different worlds in the years directly ahead of us.

One crystal ball seems to show a reasonable world full only of reasonable people, in which we say to the Russians, the Chinese and the Cubans, "We want to disarm." Thereupon they throw down their arms, embrace us, and hand in hand we all go off together looking for all the world like the proverbial lions and lambs cuddling down together in the same haymow.

These people are entitled to their views. In a way I envy their happy optimism. But some of us see an entirely different image in our crystal ball. We cannot seem to overlook the long record of brutalities visited by the Communist world on its own people, which resulted in death by starvation and other causes of at least 20 million Russians since the advent of communism. We retain the image of other brutalities to Finland, Poland, Hungary, and most recently Czechoslovakia. We remember the words of Lenin, who said that the United States of America would fall to the Communist world like a "ripe plum." We also recall the more recent words of Nikita Khrushchev when he told us "We will bury you." We remember the type of irresponsible foreign policy which egged the Arab nations on to play Russian roulette with the safety of the whole world in the Middle East. We fear that this type of irresponsibility could be

[2] From "Defense Requirements for the 1970's: Instant Myths," address before the Armed Forces Communications and Electronics Association, April 3, 1969, by John J. Rhodes (Republican, Arizona), member of the House Armed Services Committee. Text from Vital Speeches of the Day. 35:460-2. My. 15, '69. Reprinted by permission.

manifest in another deadly adventure, such as the one which brought about the Cuban missile crisis. We realize that the Cuban missile crisis was resolved in our favor only because our strength, as compared to the strength of the Communist world was overwhelming. That, unfortunately, is not necessarily the case today.

We also have not forgotten the fact that Yugoslavia was able to reform its "type of communism" and do so successfully, where Czechoslovakia tried and failed because of the harsh tread of the Russian soldier. What is the difference between these countries? The only difference was that Yugoslavia had the physical facilities to put up a creditable fight, and had indicated unmistakably that she would do so. Czechoslovakia, on the other hand, had neither the physical force nor the moral conviction to do anything but succumb to the will of the master. These lessons of recent history, unfortunately, have been lost on many of our people. In the past, this nation has been able to maintain physical force which acted as a deterrent to any enemy. Its existence was real, and its credibility was undoubted. Now, the credibility of this deterrent is threatened. The threat does not come from a lack of ability on our part to stay well ahead of the Communist world in technology, know-how, and in the use of the products of that technology and know-how. Instead, will come, if it comes, from a malaise which has attacked our people. The symptoms manifest themselves in this way:

1. The Russians are really "good guys" and if you don't "bug" them, they will not hurt you. The Chinese are really the bad guys.

2. All defense is irrelevant. The only relevance is the expenditure of huge sums of money to allow everyone to enjoy the good life now.

The people who believe that the Russians are good guys have been with us a long time. It is easy to understand them. Their numbers are dwindling, as it becomes more and more apparent that the Russians have not changed their spots, and that they are the same old leopards of the days of Stalin

and Khrushchev. However, the people infected with the mal
aise described in number 2 really create a new problem.

I suppose there is no one in this room who would no
welcome enthusiastically any cogent scheme to end povert
everywhere forever. Naturally we would like to do this. W
abhor some of the conditions we see in our core cities. W
know there is malnutrition in the country, largely caused b
ignorance rather than lack of food and fiber. There is lac
of education and lack of training. We long to get at thes
problems and to solve them. Solve them we will. The har
thing to understand is the cavalier manner in which th
victims of this malaise completely dismiss the threat to ou
national security in their zeal to solve our domestic problem:
We eternally hear complaints by people that we are "spen
ing too much money on defense, and not enough on elim
ination of poverty." I suggest that comparing these two type
of expenditures is about as sensible as comparing horses wit
rabbits or apples with oranges. They are completely di
similar, each is necessary in its own way, and each must b
pursued.

How anyone can feel, however, that the long-run benef
of the rich or poor American can be served by national weal
ness in the face of aggression is utterly beyond me. Are thes
people really oblivious to the fact that national weakne
would result in substituting slavery for what they call po
erty? Are they really unaware that the American system
which has put us in a position to dream the dreams of pove
ty elimination would be done unto death by conquest fro
without ending the dream forever? Do they really not u
derstand that even those who live in our core cities are bett
off than the great majority of workers in any other natio
in the world today? Would they really like to exchange th
lot of even our disadvantaged persons for the less palatabl
existence of the average citizen in Communist countries?

Many people will say, "Let's negotiate." I agree that w
should do this, and we will. However, experience teach
again that negotiation from a position of weakness leads onl

o defeat and disgrace—negotiation from a position of
trength leads to just and honorable decisions which can be
ved with by all parties. Let's speak softly, but let's carry at
east a sufficient stick so that our soft words may not be mis-
aken for physical or moral weakness.

You see what I am saying: The defense programs of the
eventies—and the world's history in the seventies *and* the
ighties—will to an important degree be determined by the
ontest between those two views for the minds of our citizens.

Now as our people evaluate the threats from abroad,
hey'll be influenced by their views as to the performance
f our defense officials and our defense programs including
f course the performance of defense contractors.

These days a great deal of criticism is being leveled at
he performance of defense programs. In the process we're
eeing the creation of Instant Myths. By Instant Myths, I
nean the generation of stories that "everybody knows are
rue"—except they happen to be wrong—dead wrong. In the
est of our time today, I want to discuss two of these Instant
Myths:

1. All defense contractors are profiteers who are making
oo much money!

2. Electronic contractors don't give the Government what
he contracts specify!

There are others, but those are two of the worst. You
now, and I know, that those statements simply are not true.
`oo many people believe them though; that is part of our
roblem. Let's consider these two myths a bit more fully.

First, are defense contractors profiteers gouging Uncle
am?

The myth is grounded in various allegations, each of
which is misleading or untrue.

One allegation asserts that a GAO [General Accounting
ffice] study showed that actual profits on defense contracts
ose some 26 per cent after the Pentagon began to use weight-
d guidelines. The fact is that the GAO study wasn't even
lking about actual profits. It covered only the contractors'

projected profits, before they even signed the contracts. We
all know that projected profits before a contract is started
are seldom borne out in the actual profits. More on that in a
moment. For now we simply note the untruth of the allegation that a GAO study has shown an increase of any 26 per
cent in actual profits. That story is simply untrue.

Most of our citizens are unaware of the Renegotiation
Board and its duties. As all of you know, it is the business
of the Renegotiation Board to make certain that defense
contractors do not profiteer. They have the function of post-
auditing defense contracts, and in the event that an uncon-
scionable profit is made, they have the power to force the
contractor to reimburse the Government.

As a matter of fact, the return to defense contractors has
gone down considerably in the last thirteen years. In 1956
the Renegotiation Board figures indicate that profits for defense contractors totaled $1.89 billion, or 6.3 per cent of
the sales. Ten years later in 1967, profits were down to $1.17
billion, and the rate of profit was 3.54 per cent. In 1968, sales
were at almost $39 billion, but the rate of profit was still
only 4.34 per cent.

In fact, the Congress and the Defense Department should
be worrying about attracting the most talented companies
and consortia for defense business. In many instances, our
best-equipped industrial groups can make far more profit in
producing for the private market than they can by expend-
ing a comparable effort for the Government. I certainly am
not indicating that profits have gotten down to the point
that this fear is a real and present one, but I certainly do
indicate that it is an element to be considered in determining
future Government policies.

Myth two has blossomed before our eyes in the recent
past. It asserts that defense contractors don't deliver what
their contracts specify; it goes on to assert that electronic
firms are especially guilty. . . . When we look at the facts
we find that they reflect credit, not blame, on electronic
companies.

Few industries have made such great progress in achieving reliability. The Bell System, for example, designs equipment for use in its trans-Atlantic circuits to perform flawlessly for twenty years without any maintenance whatever; and the performance exceeds the design. . . .

We have come to expect such tremendous feats from our engineers that we have become blasé. However, we really ought to stop and reflect on the electronic reliability involved in Apollo 8 and Apollo 9. Are we so blasé that we dismiss entirely the reliability involved in these shots? Let's remember they involved sending men from here to the far side of the rapidly moving moon and back to a rapidly moving earth which itself had moved millions of miles, here to splash down within a mile of the target spot—without even using the built-in corrective factors!

We ought to give the electronic industries great credit for the progress they have made. Instead they are being attacked for alleged faulty reliability.

One main reason for these attacks is the fact that the electronic industries are among the few which have quantified their reliability. Their engineers, in a quest for perfection, have found ways to measure reliability, ways to specify reliability, and ways to insure that the customer actually gets reliability. I am told that the electronic industries have gone further. They have developed parts specifications designed to give customers whatever degree of reliability they want and are willing to pay for.

One last illustration is reconnaissance equipment to allow the military to obtain as much information as possible about enemy locations and activities with a minimum of risk. Existing equipment could not solve the problems presented by the war in South Vietnam. One of the most useful items for this task is infrared reconnaissance equipment which produces imagery of the terrain overflow by an aircraft.

I've recently seen a diagram showing the performance of the best such equipment available in 1963 compared to what's now available. The improvement in these five or six years has been forty to one! ...

Now, in summing up, we need to ask ourselves some questions.

You and I know that these myths are untrue. It is not true that defense contractors are profiteers. It is not true that electronic contractors fail to live up to their contracts. Yet, many members of Congress sincerely believe these myths, and others almost as far from the facts. Why?

May I suggest that your industry has not told its story adequately? I suggest too, that many of us on Capitol Hill would welcome visits from our constituents, especially when we're at home, to give us the facts on matters like these. We get surprisingly few visits from businessmen like yourselves, and we'd welcome more. Of course, we're all very busy, but we know we must have facts if we're to vote wisely. We want to vote wisely, so bring us the facts!

THE ASSAULT ON AMERICAN INDUSTRY [3]

The military-industrial relationship that we hear so much about in this country was not invented in 1968 or 1969. It's existed for nearly two hundred years, but it's only become a significant factor with the advent of sophisticated weapons systems which demand the closest teamwork between industry and the Government.

That teamwork has meant much to this nation's security.

Yet, despite the high priority we all place on national survival, the defense industry today is being subjected to incredible denunciation. The attack has a violence unparalleled in American history.

Although some of the provocative headlines would have us believe otherwise, most Americans do *not* believe that large corporations are inherently evil, or that preparation for defense is *of itself* immoral.

[3] From address by Robert Anderson before Commonwealth Club, San Francisco, July 10, 1970. *Vital Speeches of the Day*. 36:655-8. Ag. 15, '70. Reprinted by permission. Mr. Anderson is president and chief operating officer of North American Rockwell Corporation.

Yet so vehement have been the attacks, that many sincere people are troubled when they read of excessive profits, cost overruns, lack of Government control over expenditures, and so on.

We have a twofold danger facing us in the continued harangue by those who oppose this relationship. The first is the undermining of public confidence in the integrity of defense procurement. The other is the destruction of morale of the dedicated men and women who are part of the Defense Establishment—whether in Government or industry.

The critics have had the field to themselves, confident that there would be no vigorous opposition, and hoping that there would be just silent acceptance of the charges.

To refute that thought is the reason I'm here today. This is the right time and the right audience—American businessmen who can form a serious judgment, not on what is spectacular, but on what is factual.

I can't be entirely objective in my approach, for North American Rockwell is one of the nation's major aerospace contractors and was recently awarded the very large air force B-1 weapons system contract.

However, I do believe there are two factors that enable me to take a broad view of the entire controversy. First, North American Rockwell is one of the major aerospace companies that is substantially engaged in both commercial and Government activities. Also, in my own case, because I came from the automotive industry less than three years ago, I believe I can view the matter with a new perspective.

Aerospace represents a great portion of American industry. There are 1.2 million people employed in building this country's military and commercial aircraft, its defense missiles, its space vehicles, its advanced guidance systems and its rocket engines. It's the largest manufacturing employer in the nation.

Aerospace in 1969 had sales of more than $28 billion. Its export sales of more than $3.1 billion made it the biggest industrial contributor to our balance of payments.

The opponents of this business, which has contributed so much to the military security and the economic growth of the country have rallied around the phrase, "The military-industrial complex," giving the words an accusatory ring. . . .

It is essential to keep in mind that the role of the military-industrial complex is not in *making* public policy, but in carrying it out. Viewed in that respect, industry and Government must work together toward common goals. It would be a national disgrace *if they did not.*

Fortunately, the two have always worked together and practically all of us in this room have been witness to the results.

You remember the morning of April 12, 1942, when Jimmy Doolittle lifted the first of his B-25 bomber squadron from the decks of the carrier Hornet and headed for Tokyo. How do you assess the value of Doolittle's bravery combined with the military-industrial effort that placed those bombers at the right place, at the right time?

Perhaps some of you were in the B-17 bombers flying over Germany when the first of the P-51 Mustang long-range fighters drew alongside to afford protection. Who can correctly assess the contribution of the industry that developed the aircraft which helped turn the tide of the air war?

We do not confine our security contributions to aircraft alone. Many of you remember the strident urgency of 1954, 1955, and 1956 when it became known that this nation could very well be on the receiving end of Russian nuclear intercontinental ballistic missiles.

We had the Atlas ICBM propulsion system ready—on time; we had the Thor intermediate ballistic missile propulsion system ready—on time.

These achievements and events are fresh in our minds yet we are witnessing today, with these continuous unwarranted attacks on our defense industry, a gradual erosion, a weakening of this nation's defense posture. That is a matter of grave concern. . . .

Let's look at some of the charges.

One of these pertains to the size of the defense and aerospace industry. "Most of the big military contractors," they say, "could not survive without weapons business"—with the implication that corporations are influencing defense expenditures.

True, there are a handful of major aerospace companies almost entirely devoted to Government work. However, according to Moody's Industrials, the defense portion of the twenty-five largest prime defense producers in 1969 accounted for *less than one seventh* of their total business. Most aerospace companies are becoming increasingly diversified, with a wide range of commercial and industrial endeavors. Typically, they subcontract half of their prime contracts.

Let me assure you that American industry *can* survive without the so-called "crutch" of defense spending. Nevertheless, the defense industry *is* being hurt badly by the ceaseless attack on the integrity of its highly skilled employees who see years of dedicated effort being dismissed as of no importance or as of outright moral harm.

Another belief propagated is that spending for aerospace and defense needs has grown during the past five or six years at the expense of providing for health, income security, aid to the poor, education, and other social programs.

First, let me emphasize that it is the elected representatives of the people, and not industry, who rightfully set national priorities.

The significance of congressional-established national priorities was stated with great clarity last December by Dr. Arthur Burns, now chairman of the Federal Reserve Board, who said,

> The explosive increase of Federal spending during (the decade of the sixties) is commonly attributed to the Defense Establishment, or more simply to the war in Vietnam.
> The fact is, however, . . . that civilian programs are the preponderant cause of the growth of the Federal budget. When we compare the budget of 1964 with the estimates for this fiscal year, we find that total Federal spending shows a rise of $74 billion, while defense outlays are larger by only $23 billion. . . . Thus, the

basic fiscal fact is that spending for social programs now dominates our public budgets.

Dr. Burns' comments are underscored by the fact that in this current fiscal year, we will spend less on defense as a percentage of our gross national produce—7 per cent—than in any one year in the past twenty years.

Today, an estimated 36 per cent of the Federal budget is allocated for defense—this is in contrast with the 61 per cent in 1952.

More than half of the defense budget of $77 billion is for personnel and operating costs. Military personnel costs this year are around $23 billion. Another $22 billion goes to operations and maintenance. Less than half is used to procure equipment and services from industry.

Moreover, in those declining percentages there is a hidden fact that could spell acute danger for this nation.

This country is in second place behind the Soviet Union in the development of new weapons system. Let me repeat, *we are behind* the Russians at this moment.

The Soviet Union has invested the equivalent of $16 billion this year in defense-related research, development and applications. What has the United States allocated? Thirteen billion dollars—three billion less than the Soviet Union.

Those figures, by the way, are taken from statements by Dr. John S. Foster, Director of DOD's [Department of Defense's] Defense Research and Engineering.

Continuation of that downward trend, spurred by these relentless attacks, is a direct threat to America's long-time confidence that it can meet any challenge in defense, in atomic energy, or in space.

What adds to the seriousness of this lagging research and development effort is the certainty that never again will we have the luxury of time to catch up if an enemy attacks. Never again will we have the nearly two years between the invasion of Belgium and the sinking of the Lusitania. Never again will we have a year and more between the Battle of Britain and the disaster at Pearl Harbor.

Defense-related research and development is a vital activity.

However, the critics are suspicious of any activity, including research and development, because of what they contend are the "fat profits" in aerospace participation.

What *is* the profit picture?

The most penetrating and exhaustive analysis of corporate profits was a study by the Logistics Management Institute, a nonprofit organization, which compared the profits of 40 companies substantially engaged in defense production, with 3,500 companies not engaged in defense.

The results of this broad-based analysis showed that profit on sales for the commercial and industrial companies was almost double that for defense-related works, and profit on investment in nondefense efforts, since 1963, was 40 per cent to 74 per cent greater. . . . [For a critical assessment of the Institute's study, see "Military Procurement," in Section II, above.]

Related to this matter of profits is another popular myth about the supposedly low risk involved in aerospace programs. The critics would have the public believe there is no risk in advancing the frontiers of technology; or to the extent there *is* risk, that the Federal Government underwrites all the risk involved in space and defense programs.

Again, the facts just do not support this belief.

Until recently, when there was a change in the contract ground rules, financial risk had shifted so heavily to the industry side that a company could be betting its corporate existence that it would be able to remain afloat while producing the goods or services required by the Government.

As an automotive man, I was amazed by my first encounter with the total package procurement concept.

The fixed-price total package procurement process embraces the entire span of a program from concept through development, into production. The concept was supposed to eliminate both schedule slips and unpredictable cost increases. Further, it was intended to balance the contractor's

commitment along the thin line between appropriate financial risk, on the one hand, and catastrophic corporate loss
on the other.

In practice, the concept not only delayed the procurement of many needed systems and equipment, but it also
fostered an utterly unrealistic budgeting process. . . .

Can you imagine an automobile manufacturer contracting at a fixed price to deliver a model 1977 automobile six
years from now? And an automobile, let me add, is infinitely
less complicated than a modern weapons system.

That's exactly what was asked of the aerospace industry.

Those much publicized cost overruns were not synonymous with waste; neither were they a symbol of excessive
profits. Rather they were the surface reflection of the cost
uncertainties inherent in developing and manufacturing
advance systems.

No business is ever perfect, of course, but what is never
captured in the blazing headlines of cost overruns is the
reality of endless changes, of inflation, of the costly impact
of solving problems which could not be foreseen. These are
the realities which accompany the advancement of technological frontiers. . . .

We're not trying to stamp out constructive criticism. We
expect it; we can learn from it. But we are entirely opposed
to the extremists who aim, not at correction, but at destruction. They want to disband our Military Establishment, and
abandon our defense-related capacity.

John Kenneth Galbraith, for example, has stated that
the solution of all our ills is nationalization of the defense
industry.

What would be the consequences of nationalization?
Another post office operation? In July 1969 *Fortune* magazine said: "There is some danger that the generally competent and innovative American aerospace industry could
become simply a job shop to Government." "The companies," *Fortune* said, "could end up in the situation of the
old-fashioned American shipyards, which relegated the de-

sign function to the navy's former Bureau of Ships or to outside naval architects, and thereby lost the production efficiencies that accrue when designs are drawn with producibility in mind."

To me, nationalization would be national disaster, and I believe the best answer to Mr. Galbraith was the silence that greeted his proposal.

In this troubled world beset by man-made problems in population, in transportation, in housing, in communications, and in pollution, there is need for exactly the type of expertise demonstrated by the aerospace industry during this past year in America.

The problems facing us are gigantic, nationwide, even worldwide in scope. Their solution will require technical skill and management skill of the highest order. The best management, in terms of inventiveness is in the industry that has built the world's foremost supersonic, trisonic, and hypersonic aircraft; the industry that has developed "miracle" guidance systems; the industry that has ringed this nation with defensive ICBMs, and bridged the gap to the moon.

But I do not want to leave you with the mistaken impression that we stand now as pillars of strength ready to take on all adversaries. We have been hurt by this endless tirade of abuse, and all of us in business must act vigorously to overcome this constant erosion of American defense capability.

We are determined to resist that erosion.

Our positive refutation to the strident, uninformed voices will be our continuing effort to furnish the most efficient and effective systems required for the defense of this nation.

This nation *must* continue its technological leadership. To default, to let that leadership slip away to Russia without further protest, means the passive acceptance of major risks in our national security.

And without security all else is fruitless.

SOME CONCERNS ABOUT NATIONAL SECURITY:
DANGEROUS TIMES [4]

I believe our country is in greater danger today than at any time in its history. Despite the fact that it is faced with the most powerful enemy it has ever had, it is now, incredibly, engaged in disarming.

Our people appear unaware of their peril and there is an alarming paralysis of leadership. We have no Churchill or Lincoln with the vision and courage to warn and unite our citizens to the effort required for survival.

It is my hope that by sharing my concerns I can enlist if not your support in remedial action, at least your thoughtful consideration of some of our problems with possible solutions. . . .

I was deeply concerned during the eight years when McNamara was Secretary of Defense, in his unilateral disarmament program, based naïvely upon the conviction that the U.S.S.R. would be happy to follow suit. I thought when it was initiated that it was unsafe and unwise and subsequent events have completely verified this estimate.

At the time of the Cuban missile crisis our strategic superiority was four or five to one. The Kremlin had no alternative but to comply with President Kennedy's ultimatum.

The Politburo learned that lesson well, threw Khrushchev out, and began at once an all-out effort to gain strategic superiority. This they have now achieved. Secretary of Defense Laird recently told a congressional committee that Russia's nuclear delivery capability was at least twice that of the United States in megatonnage. It is long since evident that the Kremlin is not satisfied with strategic parity, since they continue to improve their strategic posture at forced draft.

In this situation the critical question is: What will the President, our Commander in Chief do? Is he aware of the

[4] From an address by Lieutenant General Ira C. Eaker, USAF (retired) delivered before Air War College graduating class, June 5, 1970. Text from *Vital Speeches of the Day.* 36:702-4. S. 1, '70. Reprinted by permission.

loss of our strategic superiority and what will he do about it? When he was a candidate for the presidency, Mr. Nixon's campaign speeches expressed grave concern about Russia's growing strategic strength coincident with our unilateral disarmament. It has surprised me therefore that the process of U.S. disarmament has accelerated under the first two Nixon budgets.

This is my present analysis of the Nixon defense policy:

He will go to the country this fall, in an effort to elect a Republican Congress, by reminding our people that he expressed the hope that we are leaving a period of confrontation with the Reds and moving into a period of negotiation. Since he became President, therefore, he has reduced our defense budgets by more than $10 billion and has not deployed a single offensive strategic weapon, relying upon SALT [Strategic Arms Limitation Talks] to provide for our continued security through negotiation. In the meantime, Mr. Nixon will continue to wind down the Vietnam War, reducing by more than half the extent and cost of that conflict and reducing our armed forces by about one million men, military and civilian.

Whether this plan will be politically effective, resulting in Republican control of Congress, I cannot say, not being a politician or political commentator. But I am certain, having spent fifty years as a Red watcher, that it will not favorably influence Kremlin policy. The U.S.S.R. will never agree to return to strategic inferiority or parity at Vienna or anywhere else. There is no evidence that they have abandoned their plans for world domination and they know that parity is not the route to success in that area.

Instead of the period of negotiation, for which the President hopes, we shall, I believe, have a period of Red nuclear blackmail. Taking advantage of their strategic superiority, the Reds will begin to show their muscle and make hostile demands. Already since achieving superiority they have become much more aggressive. Their air and sea bases in North Africa, their missiles and fighters in Egypt, their growing naval thrusts into the Mediterranean Sea and Indian Ocean provide unmistakable evidence of this. . . .

Faced then with positive evidence of Red truculence and blackmail, President Nixon will go to the American people in his own reelection bid in 1972 reminding our people and all the world that he bent over backward in an effort to support SALT. He even continued our own strategic disarmament for two years despite certain evidences of the Red strategic arms build-up. Since this effort failed, he proposes to begin at once to restore the strategic imbalance. He can point out that since we have twice the economic resources of the U.S.S.R. we can and will do this without further delay. Such a campaign promise will be very effective as our people will by then have ample warning of the hazard in strategic inferiority, the loss of the credibility of our deterrent posture.

There is a danger in the Nixon defense strategy as I have outlined it. The Reds may not permit our rearmament. Over the Hot Line from Moscow could come this ultimatum: "As you know, Mr. President, we now have your land-based ICBMs [Intercontinental Ballistic Missiles] well covered with our SS9s. Your own Secretary of Defense has told your Congress that we can destroy 95 per cent of your ICBM capability in a surprise first strike. The only thing we now have to fear is your Polaris and Poseidon nuclear submarines. We now order you to send these vessels into the Black Sea where we can be sure they are disarmed. You will be wise to comply, since each of your subs at sea is now tailed by two of our killer subs which can destroy your ships at will."

In such a circumstance, when the U.S.S.R. has about the same strategic superiority, four to one, which we enjoyed at the time of the Cuban missile crisis, the President will have no alternative but to comply with the Red ultimatum as Khrushchev responded in 1961.

What can be done to avoid such a tragic surrender?

First, at least half of our bomber force must be on airborne alert at all times. This bomber force must be mod-

ernized by the early development of the B-1 including its
decoys and missiles.

Next, the Minuteman III and MIRV [Multiple Indiv-
idually-Targeted Reentry Vehicle] program must be pushed
at maximum effort.

Then these more long-range steps must be taken, but initiated now:

The AWACS (Air Borne Warning and Control) system
must be expedited.

We must make our land-based ICMs [Interceptor Mis-
siles] mobile, putting them on trucks as the U.S.S.R. is now
doing.

The Navy's recommendation for faster, quieter submarines must be approved.

In the meantime the ABM deployment must be expedited. It is obvious that such a system improves the credibility of our deterrent posture. The Reds believe in ABM
[Anti-Ballistic Missile missile] effectiveness. They continue
to develop and deploy such a system.

High on our priority list must be the rehabilitation of
our Air Defense Command, including the earliest possible
deployment of an interceptor like the F-12, capable in performance and in numbers of dealing with the Red bomber
force. For the first time it now exceeds our own bomber
capability. They now have two or three hundred heavy
bombers capable of reaching any U.S. target and seven hundred medium bombers which can reach any U.S. target with
air refueling and they have such refueling capability. The
U.S.S.R. also is now flight-testing a supersonic bomber like
our proposed B-1.

Our own bomber force, as all of you know, numbers
450 B-52s now twenty years old plus 150 F-111s, medium-
range bombers which are grounded.

One of the most effective measures to restore the credibility of our ICBM deterrence would be to devise a system
for automatic launch, sometimes called launch on warning.
If an enemy knew that when his ABMs were launched it

would trigger the release of our own and that the SS9s would hit empty silos, there would be little prospect that even a madman like Hitler would try a preemptive attack.

All the evidence suggests that the U.S.S.R. is making an extensive effort in space weapon capability. To their FOBS [Fractional Orbital Bombardment System] capability has lately been added the launch of a space weapon capable of destroying our reconnaissance satellites. Without our spy satellites our warning vanishes and our deterrent capability entirely disappears. We then become the "helpless, blind giant," recently referred to by President Nixon.

The United States must develop a space capability to overhaul, inspect, and, if need be, destroy any enemy space weapon or satellite.

Perhaps our greatest present deficit vis-à-vis the U.S.S.R. is in research and development. The U.S. program in R&D has become less and less, year by year and it is now considerably inferior, by any measurement, to that of the U.S.S.R. This assures the dismal prospect that in the years ahead the Reds will have strategic weapons of superior quality. Herein probably lies our greatest future danger.

With budgets at present levels, each of the armed services must review their weapons needs and establish priorities. These priorities must be coordinated at the JCS [Joint Chiefs of Staff] and DOD [Department of Defense] levels to insure that they mesh, are reciprocal and eventually will cover the whole security spectrum without duplication.

I am aware, of course, as you probably are, that few if any of these courses of action I have suggested as necessary to regain and retain the credibility of our deterrent strategic posture can be taken in the present political climate in this country.

We are now tragically and incredibly, for the first time in our history, witnessing large-scale treason. A traitor traditionally is one who knowingly gives aid and comfort to the enemy. A considerable number of our citizens, some in high places, have been engaged in treasonable acts and statements for some time. They hide behind the legal fiction that we are engaged in an undeclared war and there is therefore no official enemy.

I believe that when some historian of the future does the job on us which Gibbon did on Rome he will find that the first certain evidence of our decline was our tolerance of treason.

Another popular and political manifestation inimical to the national security is the attack on the Military Establishment and its people. The left-wing spate of invective and antipathy against the so-called military-industrial complex and the demand of many college presidents, faculty members and campus revolutionaries that ROTC be eliminated are two other very dangerous manifestations of this condition.

The determination of pacifist groups and congressional "doves" to reduce defense appropriations and deny needed new weapon systems is but further evidence of the dangerous political and popular climate in which we live today. While some of this is, of course, Communist inspired and agitated by the traitors I mentioned earlier, many patriotic citizens simply do not believe that the Reds represent a menace to our present and future security.

In earlier times since World War II, whenever our defenses were at low level and military appropriations were reduced dangerously, the men in the Kremlin always came to our rescue. They invariably made some offensive gesture or took some definite hostile action to warn our people and our leaders of their hazard. Greece, the blockade of Berlin, Korea, the Cuban missile crisis and the invasion of South Vietnam fall in this category.

Some observers feel the present Soviet leaders are too smart to make that mistake now. I do not agree. I think they are showing more truculence, more muscle and less evidence of a desire for peaceful coexistence and accord than at any previous time. Their expanding fleets in the Mediterranean Sea and Indian Ocean, their missile ships sailing into the

Caribbean, their bombers in Cuba and their missiles and fighters in Egypt, give ample evidence of aggressive designs.

The new factor in this warning process is that Russian aggression no longer worries U.S. leaders or disturbs the American people. Those who urge us to continue unilateral disarmament really do not believe the Reds represent a threat to the United States or to Free World security.

Now we come to the crux of the matter. What can we who realize our hazards do to awaken our people to their peril?

Military men have a dual responsibility. They must, of course, maintain the highest professional competence. They must at all times be prepared to execute any mission directed by the Commander in Chief despite any private opinion or personal hazard.

In addition they must exercise maximum influence to acquaint their fellow citizens with all pertinent facts concerning the strategy, tactics and weapons essential to that security. It is in this area I think we of the military have been most remiss in recent years. I credit McNamara's extraordinary effort to muzzle the military with much of the silence and detachment of men in uniform during the last few years. But McNamara is gone, fortuitously, and leaders of greater wisdom, and sounder judgment have replaced him. Military men can regain their citizenship.

In earlier times when we had only a few thousand military officers we made a much greater effort and were much more successful in communicating with our people on all aspects of national security. If we do not return to this effort, achieve greater success and obtain more support and resources for the defense mission we shall not have the weapons, the forces, the budget and the popular support requisite to a safe defense posture.

I am doing all that I can in this area, more than at any time in my life, since the need is now infinitely greater, and I exhort each of you wherever you are and in whatever way you can to inform and influence our people about what must be their number one concern, the credibility of our defense posture, the security of our country.

I regret that I have not delivered a more cheerful message today. But these are not happy days. They are dangerous times. They call for extraordinary concern and involvement by all patriotic citizens and demand the careful selection of courageous leaders.

The air force is not the only military element in our defense system, of course. The land and sea approaches must be protected as well as the air and space frontiers. But there can be no credible deterrent defense posture without an effective aerospace force. For that reason I shall be hoping and praying for your complete success in your future professional careers. As you its future leaders go, so goes the air force. As the air force goes, so goes the national security.

WILL INTERNAL DISSENT DESTROY NATIONAL SECURITY? [5]

Reprinted from *U.S. News & World Report.*

Q. General Wheeler, what is your main concern about our military situation right now?

A. My main concern, above all others, is the attitude of the country toward the American military.

Q. What attitude? Do you mean hostility?

A. I do, indeed. The fact of the matter is that this hostility toward the American military—toward the so-called military-industrial complex—has reached such a stage that military people are debarred from going on some campuses for the purpose of recruiting young men for military service.

We find that some colleges are refusing to engage in defense-research projects. This is to the detriment, I believe, not only of the scientific community, but certainly to the detriment of the security of the United States.

[5] From "Why Defense Planners Worry," interview with General Earle G. Wheeler, chairman of the Joint Chiefs of Staff. *U.S. News & World Report.* 68:34-9. Ap. 20, '70.

This hostile atmosphere, which I fervently hope is a passing phase, causes young men to be reluctant to engage in military careers. I do not think this is good for the United States. I know it's not good for the American military.

By and large, this hostility is my greatest concern at the present time.

Q. How do you account for this? Is it a result of Vietnam?

A. It's only partly Vietnam. I think Vietnam is a convenient peg to hang it on. But it probably goes deeper than that. I even have the idea that this is an organized effort, at least some of it. I don't mean that everybody who is against the American military and is going out trooping through the streets throwing rocks through windows is a Communist agent or Communist-inspired. I don't believe that at all. But I certainly think that it's more than mere coincidence that this kind of thing is going on.

If there had never been a Vietnam, you would still have this same type of attack going on against the established organs of government. That's my opinion. I am led to believe that there is a concerted effort to tear down the fabric of the Government.

Q. Is it inspired from outside the country to any degree?

A. I'm certain that people outside the country are probably contributing to it, but I couldn't document that in any way.

Q. Under these circumstances—when you have an atmosphere such as you describe—what are the chances of raising an all-volunteer Army in this country?

A. This is precisely one of the problems. The Gates Commission report specifies that we can go to an all-volunteer Army by 1 July 1971. I am strongly in favor of increased volunteering for our armed forces, but how can you raise an all-volunteer force in that short a time, with the atmosphere of the country being what it is?

Q. Does this atmosphere make it difficult to retain qualified people in the services?

A. That is another of the problems. You take a young officer or a young soldier—they are subjected to pressures and influences the same as anyone else. Nobody wants to be regarded by his fellow citizens as being unfit for human society, and to be shunned because he wears a uniform. So the tendency among some young men is to just get out—to quit. All of the services are having serious retention problems.

In other words, it's not merely the acquisition of recruits that is important; it's retaining the man who has had one hitch or two hitches, who has been trained with great care and some expense in some hard skill. All of a sudden he leaves. He's got to be replaced. You've got to train somebody else to take his place. This is a real loss to the service and to the country.

Q. Where is all this likely to lead, if there isn't a change in these attitudes?

A. I would say it is going to lead to chaos—to disintegration of the services.

Q. General, did we have this same problem, to a greater or lesser degree, after the two world wars and after Korea?

A. We certainly had no problems such as this after World War I or World War II. And while Korea was not a popular war, we certainly didn't have the same reactions within the country that we are having now.

Q. Is this hostility toward the military shared by members of Congress?

A. Certain members of Congress appear hostile. Actually, I don't know whether it's true hostility or whether, in an effort to finance the programs which they consider to be more important, this is a very convenient way for some members of Congress to attack the whole defense budget. I believe that over the next several years our defense programs are going to have a very difficult time in Congress. This is another of the problems that we have to try to deal with.

Q. Are you generally satisfied with the money available for new weapons?

A. If we get the funding which we have asked for for various systems coming up, I think we'll be all right.

But you should remember that we haven't built a new missile launcher in some years. In other words, our strategic forces have remained static. Our shipbuilding program has been curtailed rather extensively, so that the fleet is getting overage. The Safeguard antimissile system is just aborning. We haven't built a new fighter plane—something that we badly need. And we haven't built a new bomber—a true bomber, an intercontinental bomber—since the B-52. In 1978, which is the soonest that we can have a new bomber, the youngest B-52 will be sixteen years old.

Q. What have the Russians been doing about modernizing their forces?

A. They've put at least three new fighters into the air in the time period I'm talking about. They have recently demonstrated a new medium bomber which appears to be a good aircraft. They have developed their ABM system around Moscow. They have not only very substantially increased the levels of their SS-9 and SS-11 missiles, but they are in fact installing what we call the SS-13, and are apparently working on another missile—all at the same time.

And they've built up their fleet. They have made a very substantial effort with their fleet—not only with their submarine force, but also cruisers, the *Moskva*-type antisubmarine-warfare vessel, and amphibious forces. These amphibious forces are still small—what they call marine infantry—but they have a prototype perhaps of a future larger force.

Q. General, is the military security of the country greater or less than when you became Chairman of the Joint Chiefs six years ago?

A. In the strategic nuclear field, it is quite definitely less than it was six years ago. The reason is a very substantial build-up of Soviet offensive strategic weapons. I'm speaking both of their land-based missile systems, the SS-11 and the

SS-9, and the more recent development of Polaris-type submarines.

So the relative strategic capabilities of the two countries have changed radically in the last six years.

I am not saying that I am alarmed that the security of the country is jeopardized, because as of now we're still in sound shape. I am talking about the relative capabilities of the two countries—and relatively we are not so strong as we once were.

Q. Was it inevitable that the Soviet Union should overtake the lead that the United States had six years ago?

A. Not inevitable, I would say.

What was inevitable was that they would try to close the gap, probably as a result of their experiences of 1962 in the Cuban missile affair. I think they found themselves, in retrospect, at such a decided disadvantage in the strategic field that they felt they had to do something to make the relative capabilities of the two countries more nearly equal from their point of view.

Q. Do you accept the idea that nuclear parity—with the United States and Russia fairly evenly balanced—is the best way to insure peace?

A. Not necessarily. I don't mean to imply that nuclear parity necessarily would cause an outbreak of war. But, from where I sit, I would prefer to see the United States with a "nuclear sufficiency." I prefer to see us stronger than the Soviets, if possible.

Q. Has our conventional military strength surpassed that of Russia as a result of the build-up for the Vietnam war?

A. No. Far from it. It is true our conventional power is greater than it was six years ago, because of the Vietnam build-up. However, the Soviets maintained then, and maintain today, very substantial conventional forces. They maintain something over 150 line divisions, about a third of which are what we call category I, which means that they are ready to fight right now.

We have never attempted to match the Soviets division for division, the reason being that we have depended since 1950 on collective security, mainly the North Atlantic Treaty Organization. And we have tied, you might say, our assets with those of the NATO Allies, to have enough conventional force to deal initially with a Warsaw Pact conventional attack in Europe.

Q. Are the two countries—United States and Russia—roughly equal in numbers of men under arms?

A. The two are very comparable in numbers. However, you've got to recognize that the Soviet forces and ours are not organized in a symmetrical way. Our forces are organized to fight not in the United States but overseas, whereas they —occupying the central position on a tremendous land mass —are organized differently insofar as their logistic and support units are concerned.

One result is that it costs us more men to support a force in the field than it does the Soviets. For example, we have maintenance units in the field that must have the capability to rebuild tanks, vehicles and so on. They don't have to do that.

Q. Just how has the conventional strength of the Soviet Union been growing in the last few years?

A. In numbers, it has stayed about the same; in capability, it has increased very substantially. The Soviets have mechanized their forces—tanks, armored personnel carriers. They have put in greater artillery. They have a vast number of helicopters in their forces. They have a substantial number of tactical missile launchers—I'm speaking of what we would call the Honest John type—in various echelons of their corps and even some in divisions.

Q. With new weapons systems becoming so expensive, is it possible that the United States will swing back to heavier reliance on strategic weapons and away from conventional forces—in other words, back to the Eisenhower era of "massive retaliation?"

A. We haven't yet. However, the way you posed your question, you're speaking of the future—and certainly with weapons getting to be so expensive, this could be one result. I would certainly counsel against that.

Q. Do most military men feel that way?

A. Yes, because in a strategic nuclear exchange, everybody is going to lose. There is just no question about that. I don't believe the Soviets would adopt a similar posture—even if we did.

I certainly hope we don't, because it would give the Soviets a great freedom of action to move in Europe and in Asia, more or less at will....

As it happens . . . I always have been a strong advocate of conventional forces because, people being what they are, we are going to have wars for some time to come. I would rather fight a conventional war and accept the destruction and losses that go with that than fight a nuclear war and have to accept the calamitous destruction that goes with nuclear war....

Q. General, is it going to be possible to reach an arms-control agreement with the Russians?

A. I think it may be possible to negotiate an arms-limitation agreement that would be satisfactory to the security of both countries.

For example, I think that you could postulate agreed levels of ABMs for each side. I think you could come to some agreement on numbers of launchers of various kinds—I'm not talking ABM now; I'm talking offensive weapons, numbers of submarines, systems of that nature—that would be adequate to the security of both countries.

Q. Are you satisfied that the United States could inspect and safeguard such a treaty?

A. Only in certain areas. And one of the prime requisites of any viable agreement is to make an agreement only on those elements that you can verify with high confidence.

Q. Some people have been led to believe that once multiple warheads—or MIRVs—are deployed, there will be no practical way to guarantee an arms-limitation treaty. Do you agree?

A. I know of no way, myself, where you can verify by unilateral means whether or not a weapon, under foreign control, is a MIRV weapon or not.

Furthermore, I personally have yet to be convinced that you can stop the advance of science. In other words, what you're really talking about when you say, "We'll ban MIRV," is trying to ban scientific advance. It can't be done.

Ever since the first prehistoric scientist devised the bow and arrow, military men have been trying to cope with the things the scientific community has come up with. . . .

Q. If you have an arms-limitation agreement which is limited only to what you can detect by yourself—and you know you can't detect MIRV, or multiple warheads—how much good is it?

A. I don't see why MIRV is such an important element. It's only one part of the whole package. After all, MIRV is nothing more or less than a proliferation of warheads on one missile. You can achieve exactly the same effect by building more missiles. So it doesn't have the sinister connotation that many people give to it.

I mentioned that we haven't built a single additional launcher in some years. The one offensive increase that we have made, or are making, is the creation of a MIRV weapon.

MIRV has two factors that are useful. The one that receives all of the attention is from the people who are opposed to antiballistic-missile defenses, because MIRV gives an enemy greater capability to penetrate defenses. But it also gives us more warheads to attack the target.

In other words, MIRV has two purposes—not just the one that has received at least 99 per cent of the attention.

Q. Does that mean you do not consider multiple warheads a "destabilizing element?"

A. No, I don't. Nor do I agree with those who are saying that, if we don't stop proceeding with MIRV, we'll rule out the possibility of any arms limitation. I don't agree with it at all.

In the first place, as we all know, the Soviets are testing some variety of multiple warhead. I wouldn't say that it's a MIRV in the true sense of the word, but it's certainly a multiple warhead for their SS-9s—three per missile.

I don't see why not coming to an agreement on one element of a package is going to rule out any kind of arms limitations. The Soviets haven't shown any indication along that line, so far as I am aware. . . .

Q. You mentioned earlier that we need to build up our fleet, our missile capability and various other systems. The Federal budget for the military is about $72 billion a year now. Four or five years from now, what would it cost to provide the defense that you think would be necessary?

A. I would say if we added another 10 or 12 per cent onto what we have right now, that we should be able to undertake a very satisfactory defense program. I'd say around $80 billion.

Q. Do you think it's likely that the Pentagon will get this, considering the demand for domestic spending?

A. I don't know—and that's what bothers me. The cost of weapons systems continues to be very high. The demands in the social and civil sectors have been going up much faster than the demands in the military area, as you know. I just don't know what is going to be available for the military. But, as I see it, national defense is a primary domestic need.

Q. What would the effect be if military spending went down to $50 billion or $60 billion?

A. If we go down to that level, I think all of us better start looking at our muskets on the wall and decide what we're going to do.

Q. General, as you look down the road, do you see any sunshine at all—any reason for optimism at all?

A. I'm not a pessimist by nature. Winston Churchill said he was an optimist, in light of the alternative. I am not, however, an undue optimist.

What I have found over the years is that the American people are pretty sensible. I believe that today's atmosphere isn't going to last forever. I believe also that the American people are sensible enough that they will be willing to pay the necessary taxes to provide an adequate defense for this country. I can't think that they would act otherwise.

In other words, this attitude of hostility is a passing phase. However, it will pass faster with proper action than if it is allowed simply to go along unchecked—without any reaction on the part of anyone.

A SUPERIOR MILITARY TECHNOLOGY [6]

Today, a . . . major element of basic national security policy should be the absolute determination to maintain a superior military technology in the fighting forces of the United States. This is no easy task. The first problem, if our nation had such determination, arises from the imbalance in technical intelligence opportunities which exist between the Communist world and the Free World.

Ours is an open society and most of our scientific and technical intelligence information is widely published in trade journals, in newspapers, in various periodicals, scientific works, and often is exhibited on television. The Communists, on the other hand, have a second iron curtain within their political iron curtain. This second barrier is the "technological" curtain which deliberately conceals from the rest of the world any Soviet technological progress which might have military significance.

Our Military Establishment and our defense industry consciously and constantly feed back the results of research and development programs into the consumer industry. Most of the material, metallurgical, and electronic advances of . . . [the] past twenty years have had their roots in military re-

[6] From *Neither Liberty Nor Safety*, by General Nathan F. Twining, USAF (retired). Holt. '66. p 281-3. Copyright © 1966 by Nathan F. Twining. Reprinted by permission of Holt, Rinehart and Winston, Inc.

search and development. The civilian aircraft in which we ride across the United States in four hours owes its existence to military propulsion and aerodynamic innovations. The now universally available new cooking utensils to which food will not stick while cooking, and which need no scouring, owe their development to the work which the Military Establishment did on ballistic missile reentry systems. Computer technology, electronic and communications systems, all of which support the functioning of industry, grew out of military research and development. The radar systems which control air traffic and prevent collision of civilian aircraft in flight, and which guide such civilian aircraft into safe landings in fog and bad weather, were perfected by the military. There are many other such innovations too numerous to mention.

The application of our Free World military technology to civilian life is proper and is a natural consequence of an open society. There is no such similar application behind the iron curtain.

This circumstance is what the military professional calls the imbalance of opportunity for acquiring and exchanging scientific and technological information. What it amounts to is that the Soviets have access to, and know, just about everything that this nation does while our Government has only fragmentary information on Russian programs.

If this nation were to assume that the geographic, demographic, and logistical power factors provided certain military advantages to the Soviet system, and if it were to assume that, because of this relationship, the United States should maintain superior Free World fighting forces, our Government would have identified a major problem. It would worry more about the "imbalance" in opportunity for acquiring technical intelligence. We might even call a part of the Cold War a "technological war," the winner of which could easily become dominant in world affairs. If the United States is indeed involved in a technological war, it must seek the answer to a simple question: How does the United States keep ahead, or stay even, when the enemy has access to practically all of this nation's scientific and technical information, and, in addition, has the benefits of his own innovations, and the United States has only what it produces by itself?

America therefore has "two strikes" against her in fighting the technological war of the future. If our Government further compounds this difficulty by the self-imposition of constraints on the progress of our own military technology, logic would indicate that we are creating an insoluble problem. And . . . the nation seems to be doing that, particularly as it affects U.S. space technology, U.S. nuclear technology, and the modernization of air and naval combat forces-in-being.

DEFENSE IS A JOB FOR MILITARY PROFESSIONALS [7]

[In 1969 President Nixon and Defense Secretary Melvin R. Laird named a fourteen-man panel of business and industrial leaders, including representatives of the defense industry, to examine the Defense Department and suggest changes in its organization and procedures. Heading the panel was Gilbert W. Fitzhugh, board chairman of the Metropolitan Life Insurance Company. The Fitzhugh Report, issued in the summer of 1970, found much wrong. The Pentagon was overstaffed by some 35,000. Billions were annually wasted by bad decisions and inefficient operations. Defense contracts, much too large, should be broken into smaller pieces, and the whole of procurement should be overhauled. Overcentralization of authority at the Defense Secretary's level impaired the decision-making process. It was recommended that the present single Deputy Defense Secretary be replaced by three. One of the three would have charge of management resources; oversee the Army, Navy, and Air secretaries;

    [7] From "In the McNamara Vein," by Anthony Harrigan, executive vice president of the Southern States Industrial Council, reporter and specialist on defense and security issues. *National Review*. 22:1110. O. 20, '70. Reprinted by permission of National Review, Inc., 150 E. 35 St. New York, N.Y. 10016.

and have charge of research and advanced technology, engineering, manpower, bases, and procurement. A second would oversee the comptroller's functions, audit contracts, and have charge of engineering and performance test evaluations. A third would be in charge of Defense Department operations. This last proposal, aimed at increasing or restoring top civilian control over military operations, at once encountered strong opposition in Congress and within the Defense Department. So did two further proposals: (a) that the Joint Chiefs of Staff and the Chairman be stripped of all operational capacity within the Pentagon while remaining heads of their own services and military advisers to the President; (b) that the present command structure be revised to establish a Strategic Command for control of strategic weapons and planning, a Tactical Command for control of general-purpose forces, and a Logistics Command to handle supplies for all services.—Ed.]

If the Fitzhugh panel recommendations are accepted by Congress (which seems unlikely), the principal result will be a new layer of civilian bureaucracy over the nation's combat forces.

One of the key proposals of the Fitzhugh committee calls for creation of an "Under Secretary of Defense for Operations." The Joint Chiefs of Staff—the general and flag-rank officers with the greatest experience in preparing for and fighting a war—would be stripped of authority for military operations. Only advisory responsibilities would be left to them. In other words, they would become figureheads.

In the place of the Joint Chiefs would be the Under Secretary for Operations, a civilian without professional military experience or credentials. This is the situation that [former Defense Secretary Robert S.] McNamara preferred and endeavored to create. Under the McNamara regime at the Pentagon, former academics even selected bomb loads for aircraft on missions over North Vietnam.

The Fitzhugh plan is further complicated—and its error compounded—by the recommendation that the Under Secretary for Operations have a single chief of staff and a staff organization duplicating the existing Joint Staff. Why one chief of staff is better than the Joint Chiefs, with their wide spectrum of experience and expertise, is not explained by the committee.

Another feature of the Fitzhugh report is a proposal for an Under Secretary of Defense for Resources. This individual would be responsible for all decisions involving military procurement and manpower. The departments of the Army, Navy and Air Force would be retained, but only as empty shells.

Consolidation of departments frequently works well in private industry. In government, merger of two or more departments usually results in a bureaucratic monster (cf. Health, Education, and Welfare). In all likelihood, the Fitzhugh recommendations for military consolidation would result in a HEW-type monster inside the Pentagon. . . .

For citizens concerned with the capabilities of the United States Armed Forces, one of the most distressing recommendations is the proposal for grouping combat forces in strategic and tactical commands. Under the Fitzhugh plan, the Strategic Air Command and the navy's force of missile-firing submarines would be under a single commander who would not be serving as the chief of a service. Everything from infantry divisions to fleet destroyers would be included in a tactical command. This was a long-sought goal of Mr. McNamara, but it makes no sense in war, because weapons systems have both strategic and tactical functions. In Vietnam, for example, B-52 bombers—designed for a strategic role—serve in a tactical support capacity. A missile-firing submarine may also be called upon to serve in an anti-submarine capacity—that is, in a tactical role. John J. O'Malley, military writer for the San Diego *Union*, rightly questions the validity of the Fitzhugh recommendation in this area, saying: "Just how wars or potential wars are to be classified neatly as 'strategic' or 'tactical,' the commission does not say."

Another unsound recommendation is the proposal for a new Defense Test Agency, under a civilian director and independent of the individual services. This also is McNamara thinking. The services should have more, not less, control over weapons testing—for the simple reason that they are the users of the weapons. Remember the F-111 fighter-bomber? The civilian bureaucrats in DOD insisted on an aircraft that they said would be suitable for both services. The navy strenuously opposed the aircraft, saying it didn't meet fleet needs, but was overruled by the civilian "experts." The final product was an aircraft that failed to please anyone.

President Nixon made a mistake when he failed to give experienced military professionals a strong voice on the Fitzhugh panel. The fact is that the real experts on defense are the men who wear the uniform of the United States and who have commanded forces in combat. Civilians from the business and/or academic communities have valuable skills to contribute to the Defense Establishment, but they aren't pros when it comes to war.

The Fitzhugh committee made numerous proposals, and each should receive careful consideration. It is apparent, nonetheless, that the committee members failed to realize that defense isn't just another business. The Pentagon isn't a corporation. The entire structure of the Defense Establishment exists for the purpose of enabling the United States to be combat-ready so it can defeat any nation or combination of nations that attacks it or threatens its interests. What is at stake in defense planning is the survival of the United States. It is imperative, therefore, that the actual control of survival forces be in the hands of skilled professionals. And it is equally imperative that the nation's armed forces be organized in ways that make sense to these soldiers, sailors and airmen.

Unfortunatcly, The Fitzhugh panel failed to recognize the need for reform along these lines. Its recommendations reflect distrust of men at arms, as revealed in the proposal to divest the Joint Chiefs of important responsibilities which they have carried out effectively in dangerous situations. In short, the Fitzhugh committee report is not a step in the direction of a stronger, more combat-ready nation.

IV. THE STRUGGLE FOR CONTROL

EDITOR'S INTRODUCTION

The basic question with which this book is concerned, the question stated in the Preface (Will we conquer this Frankenstein's monster?) remains unanswered. The prospect for an affirmative answer seems far brighter now, however, in early 1971, than it did a few years ago—or even last year. At least the question is now being asked out loud, before a wide public. There is in consequence an increasingly wide recognition that what we are faced with *is* a monster whose continued growth out of control threatens not just our freedoms but our very lives.

No longer taken at face value, either in Congress or by the general public, are the dire warnings of Communist menace issued by members of the Defense Establishment whenever a new defense budget, expanded to pay for new weapons systems, is up for congressional consideration. The warnings are now subjected to analysis to determine their solid factual content. No longer is the defense budget a sacred document, nor the Pentagon a sacred institution, veiled from eyes of the vulgar and immune to criticism. Some people suspect that members of the Defense Establishment often make policy more from interested motives than from a genuine concern for the nation's welfare. And there is a growing demand within the body politic for a return, in practice, to constitutional principles in these matters. By what right, after all, do the makers and wielders of arms make foreign and domestic policy also? Were not the Founding Fathers wise to insist, in the organic document of the Union, that the military be always and definitely subordinate to the civilian branches of Government?

The selections in this section express and record early gropings toward control of the military-industrial complex, and the grave doubts as to their efficacy and hence as to our future survival in freedom. The section opens with Herbert Scoville's flat statement that "the only solution is arms control." The selections which follow are proposals and ideas shaped by concerned men or (in the case of *Fortune* magazine's "The Case for Cutting Defense Spending") communications media. There is, however, a certain rounding out of thematic pattern in the fact that the section which opens with Scoville's statement closes with George Wald's. These two express the conviction that international arms control *is* the only answer; nuclear weapons *must* be abolished; and if we fail in our effort toward control there is no hope for the future.

INTERNATIONAL ARMS CONTROL IS THE ONLY ANSWER [1]

The spiral rises: more and more weapons, greater and greater complexity in system characteristics, greater and greater uncertainty, more and more money wasted, less and less security! The risk of nuclear war mounts every day, and the dangers from nuclear accident expand continuously. If it isn't stopped now, where will this missile madness end?

The only solution is arms control. The upward spiral must be cut now while a stable situation exists. Far better to prevent further construction of the Soviet SS-9 missiles through an arms control agreement than to try to destroy with an ABM system these missiles as they approach our cities. Far better to protect our people by controlling the size of the threat through the destruction of missiles in a disarmament bonfire than to attempt to destroy the weapons in their silos in a nuclear strike. Deterrence can be

[1] From *Missile Madness,* by Herbert Scoville (text) and Robert C. Osborn (illustrations). Houghton. '70. p 69-77. Copyright © 1970 by Herbert Scoville and Robert Osborn. Reprinted by permission. Herbert Scoville is former Deputy Director of the Central Intelligence Agency and former assistant director of the Arms Control and Disarmament Agency.

maintained with much greater certainty by agreeing to limit ABM systems than by building MIRVs [Multiple Independently-targeted Reentry Vehicles] to assure their penetration.

At the present time both the United States and Russia could agree to freeze the deployment of their forces at existing levels of current weaponry and be confident that their security would not be threatened. A freeze would leave both sides with approximately the same numbers of ICBMs. The United States would have an advantage in missile submarines and intercontinental bombers; the Soviets an advantage in shortrange missiles and in a small but ineffective ABM around Moscow. Neither nation would have an ABM system which could threaten the deterrent of the other. Further deployment of Soviet SS-9 missiles would be stopped, eliminating the threat to Minuteman. The final development and subsequent deployment of MIRVs by both nations would be forestalled by halting MIRV and MRV testing. The costly development of new advanced bombers and defensive systems to cope with them would be unnecessary.

Neither side could threaten the other or consider initiating nuclear war. Both would have overwhelming forces to deter a nuclear threat by a third nation such as China. An agreement would permit the diversion of vast resources, both men and money, to much needed internal problems. The United States might save $3-$5 billion per year over the next ten years; the U.S.S.R. a similar sum. There would be no incentives or desires to violate or abrogate such an agreement.

A major problem in all previous arms control negotiations with the Soviets has been the fear that they, because of their closed society, could violate the agreements. Today, however, the United States could verify satisfactorily the major elements of a strategic arms freeze without the requirement for on-site inspections, which have been so impossible to negotiate with the Russians. With the size of present stockpiles, the secret deployment of a few missiles would have no effect on our security. Indeed it would take hundreds or perhaps even a thousand before a violation would be significant. Without on-site inspections the United States Defense Department has for several years, been able to report the numbers of Soviet land- and sea-based missiles with great confidence. ABM deployments which could threaten our deterrent have also been observed. To build clandestinely an intercontinental bomber capable of significantly affecting U.S. security would be impossible even if there were any incentive to do so. ICBM test firings have been watched from outside Russia since 1957, and it is possible to observe without intrusion whether a missile being tested has one or several reentry vehicles.

However, once reliable and accurate MIRVs have been developed and tested, their deployment would be impossible to verify without on-site inspection unacceptable even to the United States. The external appearance of the missile will give no sign that MIRVs are present. How will it be possible to know how many warheads are contained in each missile silo? How can one confidently estimate the accuracy of each individual MIRV and the risk that it presents to our deterrent? When large-scale ABMs are deployed on a nationwide basis, it will not be possible to evaluate accurately their effectiveness even though their size is known. The threat will no longer be calculable, and agreement to halt the spiral will become increasingly difficult to obtain.

It may not be necessary to negotiate a complete freeze on offensive and defensive strategic weapons immediately. The most critical systems affecting security are the numbers of land-based missile-launchers, ABMs, and MIRVs. Only freezing the latter is really urgent because soon testing could be beyond the point of no return.

The initial agreement need not even be a formal agreement. The U.S. could temporarily cease its MIRV testing with the understanding that this halt would only continue if the Soviets exercised similar restraint. Security would not be jeopardized since the Soviets have at least temporarily halted their ABM deployment against which the U.S. MIRV was designed. Tacit understandings in which offensive missile and ABM deployments were limited could also halt the race and provide time for more enduring treaties.

But time is truly running out. *If we cannot stop this madness now, we may be dooming mankind to early extinction.* Nuclear war in the present age would mean hundreds of millions of casualties, complete destruction of our cities and modern means of existence. Both the U.S. and the Soviet Union would be the scenes of utter devastation. The effects would not halt at their borders. The repercussions throughout the world would be catastrophic.

A MODERATE'S PROPOSALS [2]

Rather than presenting the customary lambasting of the military-industrial complex, I would like to address some of the fundamental questions, as I see them, that result from the close, continuing relationship between the Military Establishment and the major supplying industries:

How can private industries be utilized for the design and production of weapon systems without converting them into unimaginative government arsenals?

How can the Military Establishment sponsor and fund most of the new product developments undertaken by these companies without assuming the role of the entrepreneur, which is so basic to the private economy?

How can the Government protect the taxpayer in its dealings with defense contractors without taking on their internal decision-making functions?

How can specialized capabilities be developed by a hard core of military suppliers without eliminating effective competition for military business?

How can the concentration of defense business in a rela-

[2] From "Military-Industrial Complex," address presented to 14th Annual Institute of World Affairs at Washington State University, Pullman, March 21, 1969, by Murray L. Weidenbaum, economist, assistant secretary (economic policy) of the United States Department of the Treasury. Text from *Vital Speeches of the Day.* 35:523-8. Je. 15, '69. Reprinted by permission.

tively few regions (and their close dependence on it) be reduced without sacrificing efficiency and effectiveness? . . .

The tendency for the development of a military-industrial complex can be reduced by changing governmental procurement policies and practices so as to halt the erosion of the basic entrepreneurial character of the firms that undertake large-scale developmental programs for the Federal establishment. The plea for "disengagement" made by defense contractors needs to be given greater weight, although the public interest necessitates continuing protection and concern. Some of the changes that I propose may sound quite technical, but they do attempt to get at the heart of the matter without disrupting vital Government programs.

If the following policy suggestions have any common characteristic it is that they are designed to reduce the close and continuing relationship between the Pentagon and a relatively small group of industrial firms. By reducing both the governmental orientation of these companies and the military's reliance on them, the nation might be able to achieve the objectives I stated at the outset of this paper—to reduce the geographic concentration of defense contracts, to increase competition for military business, to protect the interests of the taxpayer, and to reduce the arsenalization of the defense industry. That is quite a tall order and the following points are not offered as a definite solution but as important steps in the right direction.

One way of reducing the financial dependence of defense companies on the Federal treasury would be to make interest on working capital an allowable cost on military contracts. Interest on indebtedness is a standard cost of doing business and should be recognized as such. Unlike the period of rapid and uncertain expansion of defense work in the early 1940s, military contracts are now an established feature of American industry. The Treasury no longer needs to serve as banker.

A second way of strengthening the private entrepreneurial character of defense firms is to streamline and reduce the variety and scope of special provisions in procurement legislation and regulations. Let these companies develop their own safety rules to discourage employees from skidding on factory floors. We seem at times to forget why in the first place we prefer to use private enterprise rather than Government arsenals to develop and produce most of our weapon systems. It is not because private corporations are better than Government agencies at following rules and regulations—at doing it by the numbers. It is precisely for the opposite reason. We believe that private enterprise is more creative, more imaginative, and more resourceful.

A third way of reducing the close, continuing relationship between the Federal establishment and its major suppliers is to broaden the competitive base. This could be accomplished by encouraging commercially-oriented companies to consider military work as a possible source of diversification for them. The recommendations concerning interest on working capital and streamlining procurement procedures should help to make defense work attractive for the companies that are not now interested in Government work. Moreover, defense companies should be encouraged to diversify into commercial markets, as the simplest way of reducing their dependence on Government agencies. It may be natural for governmental procurement officials to favor firms whose interests are not "diluted" by commercial work. However, the diversified company may also be the more efficient one in the long run. Certainly, the diversification of industry both into and out of high technology Government markets would reduce the present tendency for a relatively small number of companies and some regions of the country to become primarily dependent on Federal business.

At present, much of the military subcontracts go to companies that are prime contractors on other systems. It is not infrequent that one of these companies . . . [competes] against . . . [others] for the prime contract for a new weapon system and, simultaneously, its electronics division teams up with one of its competitors and its propulsion system with another. Thus to cite a hypothetical but reasonable example,

Lockheed might beat out North American Rockwell and General Dynamics for a new missile contract, but assign the propulsion subcontract to North American's Rocketdyne division and the communication system to General Dynamics' Stromberg-Carlson division. Thus, the subcontracting may not necessarily broaden the array of companies participating in the defense program, but be used to "share the wealth" among the members of the club.

More attention in the award of subcontracts should be paid to small business and other industries not actively participating in the military market as primes. Some thought also should be given to reducing the competitive advantages that accrue to the major military contractors that hold on to Government-owned plant and equipment for long periods of time. The simplest approach, of course, would be to curtail the practice of furnishing plant and equipment to long-term Government contractors and, instead, to give them greater incentives to make their own capital investments.

Certainly, the detailed day-to-day governmental surveillance of internal company operations which is now so characteristic of the military market is a poor precedent to follow in establishing the future roles of industry and Government in public sector areas, both military and civilian.

On the positive side, governmental procurement of goods and services from the private sector might well emphasize the end results desired by governmental decision makers, rather than prescribing the detailed manner in which industry should go about designing and manufacturing the end product. In its essence, this is the difference between detailed design specifications prepared by the governmental buyer versus clear statements of performance desired by the Government. The latter approach, of course, gives maximum opportunity for private initiation and inventiveness to come to bear on the problems of the public sector.

That, of course, is the basic and difficult task of using private enterprise in the performance of public functions without either converting the companies to unimaginative arsenalized operations or letting them obtain windfall profits because of the Government's inability to drive hard enough and intelligent enough bargains.

ACCURATE INFORMATION—A WEAPON AGAINST PENTAGON WEAPONRY [3]

Military technology, bristling with complexity and soaring in cost, dominates the U.S. budget, yet under a dozen senators can claim a thorough grasp of modern weapons systems. To apply checks and balances to the Pentagon's monumental requests for appropriations, Senators Joseph S. Clark (Democrat, Pennsylvania [1957-1968]), Jacob K. Javits (Republican, New York), and George McGovern (Democrat, South Dakota) met with a few members of the House and proceeded to make a political invention. They founded an organization known as Members of Congress for Peace Through Law (MCPL). The privately funded group established a number of committees, one of which, Military Spending, analyzed half a dozen defense topics and last year made its first report. The Pentagon promptly dismissed it as inconsequential and poorly informed. Senator Barry Goldwater (Republican, Arizona) took to the Senate floor to criticize it.

This year [1970] the MCPL *Report on Military Spending* was taken more seriously by the Department of Defense, which managed to get its hands on one of twenty-five copies of a June 12th draft. The copying machines in the Pentagon turned out many reproductions of the report. Some turned up on the desks of members of the Armed Services Committee. One found its way to the White House. On July 16th a Pentagon spokesman targeted the MCPL report in a press conference, asserting that it contained classified data. Apparently, *now*, the MCPL group was too well informed.

[3] From "Cutting the Pentagon Down to Size," by Ralph E. Lapp. *New Republic*. 163:16-17. Ag. 22-29, '70. Reprinted by permission of *The New Republic*, © 1970, Harrison-Blaine of New Jersey, Inc.

Senator Strom Thurmond (Republican, South Carolina), standing in for Senator Goldwater, attacked the report and vowed he would keep it from being printed in the *Congressional Record*. Senator Mark Hatfield (Republican, Oregon), cochairman (with Senator William Proxmire [Democrat] of Wisconsin) of the MCPL committee on military spending, returned Thurmond's fire. Unable to pry loose a list of the violations, Senator Hatfield pinpointed an itemization that defense officials leaked to the press and documented the MCPL origin of each item. All the suspect material came from printed sources in the public domain. Two weeks after this rebuttal, Senator Hatfield met with a Pentagon spokesman and discovered that there were some thirty items of information which the Defense Department would have preferred to control, but only four serious disclosures. These, however, the official privately admitted had appeared in print elsewhere.

Staff workers who authored individual sections in the MCPL study were grieved that the Pentagon had attacked the report on security grounds. "It's a typical defense maneuver," one staffer told me, "right out of their Department of Dirty Tricks." However contrived, the DDT approach to the MCPL report backfired. Not only were the charges refuted; the controversy drew public attention to the study. . . .

After doing their homework and looking into details of the various weapons systems, the MCPL congressmen called for a $4.4-$5.4 billion cut in the fiscal year 1971 budget, along with manpower cuts amounting to about the same sum. In other words, they recommended a 14 per cent cut in military spending, which they calculated would produce "eventual savings—[of] from $95-$100 billion." The "they" in this case should be defined as eleven senators and sixteen representatives who signed the report, but it is generally viewed as including the MCPL membership of twenty-eight senators and seventy representatives.

TAXPAYER SUITS AGAINST PENTAGON
BUREAUCRATS? [4]

Defense Secretary Melvin R. Laird has sought to prevent recurrence of C-5-type fiascos [see "Report on Lockheed and the C-5A Jet," in Section II, above] by setting "milestones" which a contractor must reach before he moves on to the next phase of a weapons program. This policy means little, however, unless Pentagon bureaucrats clamp down on contractor boondoggling. Signs are thus far that they haven't. Pentagon studies already are predicting a $1 billion overrun on Lockheed's S-3A antisubmarine aircraft program, the first major weapons purchase initiated by Laird. Deputy Secretary of Defense David Packard recently succeeded in preempting headlines about that overrun by issuing a non-story that he had warned the navy to keep close tabs on program costs. Packard acknowledged only a $100 million overrun on the current portion of the contract and did not reveal the present estimate for total cost at completion.

It is too much to expect that Pentagon bureaucrats will move voluntarily to shape up military procurement. That would involve harsh measures against favored contractors and, for the less efficient among them, a bankruptcy or two. The ties that bind Pentagon bureaucrats and the giant contractors—the mutual interest in huge defense budgets, the promise of lucrative jobs in industry for former military and civilian officials, and the feeling that they must stand four-square against an unappreciative public—are simply too strong for that.

Perhaps the only answer is a series of taxpayer suits against Government officials who breach the public trust, particularly with respect to concealment of cost problems that could lead to gigantic expenditures later if not brought under control. Not too long ago, the public wouldn't have

[4] From "The Lockheed Scandal," by James G. Phillips, former military editor of *Congressional Quarterly*, author of their 1968 study on defense spending. *New Republic*. 163:23. Ag. 1, '70. Reprinted by permission of *The New Republic*, © 1970, Harrison-Blaine of New Jersey, Inc.

stood for the C-5 affair. In 1956, T. Lamar Caudle, an assistant attorney general under President Truman, was convicted and sentenced to two years in prison for failing to prosecute tax fraud cases that came under his jurisdiction. The charge on which he was convicted was conspiracy to deprive the Government "of the fair services of Caudle." That law ought to be applied to Pentagon bureaucrats.

SOME IDEAS FOR TAMING PENTAGON POWER [5]

The military power has been above challenge for so long that to attack . . . seems politically quixotic. . . . Nonetheless control is possible. I . . . offer a political decalogue of what is required. It is as follows:

(1) The goal, all must remember, is to get the military power under firm political control. This means electing a President on this issue next time. This, above all, must be the issue in the next election.

(2) Congress will not be impressed by learned declamation on the danger of the military power. There must be organization. The last election showed the power of that part of the community—the colleges, universities, concerned middle class, businessmen—which was alert to the Vietnam war. Now in every possible congressional district there must be an organization alert to the military power. . . .

This effort must not be confined to the North, the Middle West, or West. In the last five years there has been a rapid liberalization of the major college and university centers of the South. Nowhere did [Eugene] McCarthy or [Robert] Kennedy draw larger and more enthusiastic crowds than in the big southern universities. . . . Strom Thurmond [Republican, South Carolina], John Tower [Republican, Texas], and the other sycophants of the military from the South must be made sharply aware of this new constituency —and if possible be retired by it.

[5] From *How to Control the Military*, by John Kenneth Galbraith, Harvard economist, author, former Ambassador to India. Doubleday. '69. p 52-60. Copyright © 1969 by John Kenneth Galbraith. Reprinted by permission of Doubleday & Company, Inc.

(3) The Armed Services committees of the two houses must obviously be the object of a special effort. They are now, with the exception of a few members, a rubber stamp for the military power. Some liberals have been reluctant to serve on these fiefs. No effort, including an attack on the seniority system itself, should be spared to oust the present functionaries and to replace them with acute and independent-minded members. Here too it is vital that we have support in the South.

(4) The goal is not to make the military power more efficient or more righteously honest. It is to get it under control. These are very different objectives. The first seeks out excessive profits, poor technical performance, favoritism, delay, or the other abuses of power. The second is concerned with the power itself and the spending on which that power depends. The first is diversionary for it persuades people that something is being done while leaving power and budgets intact.

(5) This is not an antimilitary crusade. Generals and admirals and soldiers, sailors, and airmen are not the object of attack. The purpose is to return the Military Establishment to its traditional position in the American political system. It was never intended to be an unlimited partner in the arms industry. Nor was it meant to be a controlling voice in foreign policy. Any general or admiral who rose to fame before World War II would be surprised and horrified to find that his successors in the profession of arms are now commercial accessories of General Dynamics.

(6) Whatever its moral case there is no political future in unilateral disarmament. And the case must not be compromised by wishful assumptions about the Soviets which the Soviets can then destroy. . . . But it is wise to assume that within their industrial system, as within ours, there is a military-industrial bureaucracy committed to its own perpetuation and growth. This governs the more precise objectives of control.

(7) Four broad types of major weapons systems can be recognized. There are first those that are related directly to the existing balance of power or the balance of terror vis-à-vis the Soviets. The ICBMs and the Polaris submarines are obviously of this sort; in the absence of a decision to disarm unilaterally, restriction or reduction in these weapons requires agreement with the Soviets. There are, secondly, those that may be added within this balance without tipping it drastically one way or the other. They allow each country to destroy the other more completely or redundantly. Beyond a certain number, more ICBMs are of this sort. Thirdly there are those that, in one way or another, tip the balance or seem to do so. They promise, or can be thought to promise, destruction of the second country while allowing the first to escape or largely escape. Inevitably, in the absence of a prospect for agreement, they must provoke response. An ABM, which seems to provide defense while allowing of continued offense, is of this sort. So are missiles of such number, weight, and precision as to be able to destroy the second country's weapons without possibility of retaliation.

Finally there are weapons systems and other military construction and gadgetry which add primarily to the prestige of the armed services, or which advance the competitive position of an individual branch.

The last three classes of weapons do not add to such security as is provided under the balance of terror. Given the response they provoke, they leave it either unchanged or more dangerous. But all contribute to the growth, employment, and profits of the contractors. All are sought by the armed forces. . . .

A prime objective of control is to eliminate from the military budget those things which contribute to the arms race or are irrelevant to the present balance of terror. This includes the second, third, and fourth classes of weapons mentioned above. The ABM and the MIRV (the Multiple Independently-targeted Reentry Vehicle), both of which will spark a new competitive round of a peculiarly uncontrollable sort, as well as manned bombers and nuclear carriers are all of this sort. Perhaps as a simple working goal, some $5 billion of such items should be eliminated in each of the next three years for a total reduction of $15 billion.

(8) The second and more important objective of control is to win agreement with the Soviets on arms control and reduction. This means, in contrast with present military doctrine, that we accept that the Soviets will bargain in good faith. And we accept also that an imperfect agreement—for none can be watertight—is safer than continuing competition. It means, as a practical matter, that the military role in negotiations must be sharply circumscribed. Military men —prompted by their industrial allies—will always object to any agreement that is not absolute, self-enforcing, and watertight. Under such circumstances arms-control negotiations become, as they have been in recent times, a charade. Instead of halting the arms race they may even have the effect of justifying it. "After all we are trying for agreement with the bastards." The Congress and the people must make the necessity for this control relentlessly clear to the Executive.

(9) Independent scientific judgment must be mobilized —as guidance to the political effort, for advice to Congress, and of course within the Executive itself. The arms race, in its present form, is a scientific and mathematical rather than a military contest. Though the military can no longer barricade themselves behind claims of military expertise or needed secrecy, the opposing views must be reliably available.

So the time has come to constitute a special body of highly qualified scientists and citizens to be called, perhaps, the Military Audit Commission. Its function would be to advise the Congress and inform the public on military programs and negotiations. It should be independently, i.e., privately, financed. It would be the authoritative voice on weapons systems that add to international tension or competition or serve principally the competitive position and prestige of the services or the profits of their suppliers. It would have the special function of serving as a watchdog on negotiations to insure that the military power is excluded.

(10) Control of the military power must be an ecumenical effort. Obviously no one who regards himself as a liberal can any longer be a communicant of the military power. But the issue is one of equal concern to conservatives—to the conservative who traditionally suspects any major concentration of public power. It is also an issue for every businessman whose taxes are putting a very few of his colleagues on the gravy train. But most of all it is an issue for every citizen who finds the policy images of this bureaucracy—the Manned Orbiting Laboratory preserving the American position when all or most are dead below—more than a trifle depressing.

THE CASE FOR CUTTING DEFENSE SPENDING [6]

"Even if we are successful in eliminating the war in Vietnam," warned Melvin Laird, the Secretary of Defense, ... [in 1969] "we are still not going to come up with a drastically reduced defense budget. . . . A drastically reduced defense budget will not provide adequate security in the world in which we live." Secretary Laird presides over a U.S. defense budget of $80 billion, up 70 per cent from 1961. The likelihood of very much reduction, post-Vietnam, is very small indeed, as most Defense Department civilians and the military chiefs see it.

A growing number of critics, with long experience in the Defense Department and Budget Bureau, dispute this position. They make a strong case that post-Vietnam defense costs can be cut drastically without either damaging the national security or compromising this country's commitments to its allies. Indeed, careful analysis indicates factors other than "adequate security" are forcing up defense costs today.

The defense budget has been driven upward because much of it is based on strategic assumptions that have gone

[6] From "The Case for Cutting Defense Spending," by Juan Cameron, associate editor. *Fortune*. 80:71-3+. Ag. 1, '69. Reprinted from the August 1, 1969 issue of *Fortune* Magazine by special permission; © 1969 Time, Inc.

unchallenged since the early post-World War II years, when the enemy and his threat were quite different. The evidence is strong, too, that the force structure and force levels have been put together by the military chiefs in the absence of a clearly stated national security policy laid down by the White House. Furthermore, under the pressures of the Vietnam war, civilian control over military spending has diminished, efficiency has decreased, and a large amount of "gold plating" of the forces has taken place under the guise of meeting the needs of the war. Unless brought under control, these trends can easily drive the defense budget to more than $100 billion within a few years. In fact, the Joint Chiefs [of Staff] for the past three years have requested a budget in excess of $105 billion, and President Nixon, at the end of his campaign, foresaw defense spending, excluding the Vietnam war, rising to $87 billion by 1972.

Fortune believes that a post-Vietnam defense budget of around $61 billion would allow the United States to remain the world's No. 1 military power without any major change in its commitments, in its ability to meet military contingencies, or in its basic strategic concepts. To reach this level would require, among other things:

A cutback of the 800,000 military men, as well as the naval ships and air force tactical squadrons that have been added since the Vietnam buildup in 1965

In addition, the elimination of three and a half army divisions and three tactical air wings now deployed in Europe and Asia

A paring down of weapon systems of low-cost effectiveness, such as tactical nuclear forces and certain navy carrier units

Minor adjustments in the strategic nuclear offensive and defensive forces, principally a reduction in the B-52 bomber fleet, and dropping plans for a new intercontinental bomber

A sharp cut in funds requested by the military for modernization of weapons or improved performance, through management-control devices such as the trade-off concept—

i.e., the principle that for each additional dollar spent on procurement, a dollar must be saved elsewhere

Greater overall efficiency in the use of manpower, and a crackdown on wasteful procurement of new weapons

Clearly there is no magic number to answer the question of how much defense is enough, a question as old as war itself. The problem of deciding how much is enough is not unlike that of buying insurance. You don't buy insurance for all conceivable disasters, but only enough to cover possible losses that you cannot afford to take. The threat of potential enemies—the U.S.S.R., Red China, even Cuba— and the strategy chosen to meet these threats play an important part in the design and cost of the military forces. For example, if the country should revert to the defense posture of the Eisenhower years and cut six army divisions and six tactical air wings, the post-Vietnam budget would be around $54 billion. A post-Vietnam "minimum nuclear-deterrence" budget, which would in addition cut out portions of the nuclear striking force and tactical nuclear force, would cost only $42 billion a year. On the other hand, a "nuclear-superiority" budget, which would keep land, sea, and air forces at their present levels and provide an advanced intercontinental ballistic missile, a new strategic bomber, heavy antiballistic-missile defense, and an expanded fallout-shelter program, would run close to $100 billion. . . .

In estimating the nation's defense needs, it is important to distinguish between the strategic nuclear forces, which account for about 40 per cent of current military spending, and general-purpose forces, which account for the remainder. At one extreme, the strategic nuclear forces—the ICBMs, the B-52 fleet, the forty-one Polaris submarines, and the continental air defense—can be structured on a so-called minimum deterrence basis, or second-strike capability. Supporters of this concept argue that so long as the United States possesses, after a first strike by the U.S.S.R., the ability to inflict a very significant level of damage on the enemy in a second or retaliatory strike, that is all the nuclear deterrence we need. The rough gauge of a credible second-strike capability is power enough to destroy one quarter of an enemy's population and one half its industry, thereby effectively eliminating it as a twentieth-century power. This is the general assumption on which the U.S. strategic nuclear forces have been built since 1961.

At the other end of the scale is the doctrine of nuclear dominance in which the United States would strive for a clearly preponderant offensive capability, one superior in every way to that of the Soviet Union. In addition, there would be a major-damage limiting capability, through defensive missile strength, to prevent an enemy from inflicting an unacceptable number of fatalities or other damage on the United States in a nuclear exchange. At its extreme, nuclear superiority would give the United States a so-called first-strike capability—i.e., the ability to destroy so much of the enemy's retaliatory capacity in a surprise attack as to neutralize effectively its second-strike capability. In budget terms, the difference between these two doctrines is estimated at around $27 billion annually.

The general-purpose forces, which account for the remaining 60 per cent of the current defense budget, also provide a wide range of budget options. These forces are designed to allow the United States to control a land or sea area or deny it to the enemy in a limited war or counter-insurgency situation, as opposed to destroying an enemy's population or industry. The size and deployment of these forces are not so much related to the defense of U.S. territory as they are to the defense of other countries. . . .

The generals and admirals, in arguing for larger standing forces and more sophisticated weapons, both strategic and conventional, warn over and over again that the military threat is great and growing. They cite the growing strategic nuclear power of the Russians and the Red Chinese efforts to develop a nuclear striking force. The build-up of the Soviet Union's submarine fleet, and its growing if still modest naval surface force, plus the prototypes of a new generation of fighter aircraft, are also cited as elements of the rising threat. Military men tend to want to meet enemy forces on a one-to-one basis regardless of great differences between the United States and its potential enemies in such elements as firepower and mobility. No President since five-star General Eisenhower has been successful in forcing major reductions in the defense budget over their ceaseless warnings of imminent peril.

Outside the Pentagon, however, many of the country's civilian watchdogs of defense spending take a different view. They concede that ever since the Soviet military weakness was revealed during the Cuban missile crisis in 1962, the U.S.S.R. has been trying to close the gap between its strategic forces and the rapidly growing nuclear power of the United States. But this does not lead, they believe, to a firm conclusion that the enemy, as the military imply, is striving for a first-strike capability. Nor is there necessarily a relationship between the U.S.S.R.'s nuclear build-up and the need for the United States to maintain a conventional force of more than a million men, along with their ships, planes, tanks, and other hardware, in some four hundred major bases around the world. A former State Department official intimately connected with national security planning in the Johnson Administration says: "Our commitments and force goals associated with them, both for NATO [North Atlantic Treaty Organization] and the Far East [excluding Vietnam], account for about two thirds of our defense costs today. These commitments stem from history and not from any clear analysis of whether or not the threat that led to troop deployments in the late 1940s and 1950s is still valid." . . .

[When such analyses are made they] lead to several conclusions [as regards conventional forces]:

The U.S. forces allocated to NATO can be trimmed significantly; with their supporting components they cost today about $14 billion annually and constitute *in themselves* a more powerful fighting force than any in the world except that of the Soviet Union.

Since simultaneous attacks by the U.S.S.R. and China are a remote possibility, the two-plus contingency capability can be reduced somewhat, in the direction of the one-plus capability that existed during the Eisenhower Administration.

The U.S. Navy, which is larger than all the rest of the world's navies, friendly and hostile, put together, can be significantly reduced in size. The fleet is designed to have the capability of fighting an ill-defined mission, called "War at Sea" in defense-posture statements. Curiously, the navy's mission was given much of its present definition during the landlocked crisis of August 1961, when the Berlin Wall was built. Feeling itself hopelessly outclassed by the Soviet Union on the ground, the United States decided to offset this, in part, with an overwhelming naval force, which, in the event of future Soviet land grabs, could quickly assert and capitalize on control of the seas. This reasoning, now used in support of a $24.4-billion-a-year navy, is highly dubious.

Within the Defense Department, talk of such cuts draws angry rejoinders. An assistant to Secretary Laird snaps that those proposing large defense cuts are backing away from the strategy of collective defense that the nation adopted after World War II: "Nobody has the guts to say to hell with collective defense, and to come out and say they prefer reverting to spheres of influence. Instead they hack away at the force level, at new spending for weapons like the ABM and the MIRV, at military assistance and the financing of arms sales to friendly countries." Senator John Sherman Cooper of Kentucky, a soft-spoken Republican with wide experience in foreign affairs, however, does propose a reappraisal of collective defense.

The strategy of containment through collective-security treaties [he says] does need to be revised—even in Europe where increasingly it will be neither wanted nor needed for much longer. Countries like Thailand, Japan, and the Philippines want our forces at first, but once they have been there a while, nationalism is aroused by their presence. Whatever stability the United States has brought to the world has come, not through stationing conventional forces around the world, but through its economic aid and military assistance, and the nuclear umbrella we hold over our allies.

Cooper calls for a sharp reduction of troops stationed abroad, and a redrawing of U.S. commitments to cover the two areas he feels are most vital to the United States—Europe and Japan. . . .

The point of departure for establishing an appropriate post-Vietnam level of spending is the fiscal 1965 budget, which involved total spending authority of $50.9 billion. This is selected as a base point because 1965 was the last fiscal year before the nation's large-scale involvement in Vietnam got under way and the year in which Secretary [Robert S.] McNamara [Secretary of Defense, 1961-1968] is generally thought to have achieved the greatest management control over the Defense Establishment. This level of spending allowed the country to support a small war in Vietnam, land a force in the Dominican Republic, create a large second-strike nuclear capability, and expand as well as modernize the general-purpose forces.

By fiscal 1972, the earliest year in which most of the Vietnam costs could be eliminated, cost and wage inflation would raise the cost of maintaining and equipping an equivalent military force to an estimated $67.9 billion. The Pentagon is understood to have decided on another $10.8 billion (in 1972 prices) for procurement of newer and more sophisticated weapons. In sum, unavoidable price and wage increases, plus new weapons and equipment that the military strongly desires, would mean a fiscal 1972 budget of at least $78.7 billion. In all likelihood the spending would be significantly higher than this, since the Pentagon is anxious to retain a large part of the Vietnam augmentation in manpower. Senator Howard Cannon [Democrat] of Nevada, who sits on the Armed Services Committee, says that the Joint Chiefs have told him not to expect reduction of more than one division after Vietnam.

Fortune believes there are several areas of readily obtainable savings, which in 1972 would total $17.6 billion. Since military manpower accounts for roughly half of the total defense budget, the first step is to shrink manpower back to, and possibly modestly below, the base-line year of 1965. If the armed forces were to be cut by 1 million men from the present 3.5 million, the savings would exceed $10 billion a year.

The cuts in manpower can be achieved by eliminating the Vietnam military manpower add-on of 800,000 men and by demobilizing three-and-a-half army divisions, three tactical air wings, and some navy ships. The major cutbacks would be in army ground divisions that have been deployed in forward positions around the world for a generation like the twentieth-century equivalent of the Roman legions. Changing political conditions and the greatly increased capability in airlift (which allows 11,000 combat-equipped troops to be moved from the United States to Vietnam in forty-eight hours) argue in support of the manpower reductions. Such reductions, moreover, would lessen the great disparity between the relative defense efforts of the United States and its allies. Japan, for example, spends only 1 per cent of its gross national product on defense, and the NATO countries 5 per cent, while the United States spends 9 per cent. The United States spends nearly as much on the defense of Europe as the rest of its NATO allies combined.

The second area for defense cuts lies in introducing rigid controls over procurement to minimize the "gold-plating" of new weapons, particularly aircraft and naval ships. Deputy Secretary of Defense David Packard strongly favors the trade-off concept introduced by McNamara, which in essence says that if you buy more expensive weapons to replace existing ones, in the face of an unchanged threat, they should be more efficient—and hence fewer of them should be needed. As a hypothetical example, assume that in 1962 the air force determined it needed 1,000 fighter planes costing $3 million each. Later it comes in with a proposal to buy new planes that will cost, say, $6 million apiece. Under the trade-off concept, the Secretary of Defense might well decide to buy only half as many of the new planes, on the theory that each plane should be twice as effective. . . .

Fortune's budget assumes deployment of the controversial Safeguard ballistic-missile defense system, whose costs in 1972 are estimated here at $2 billion annually. Also included in the budget are funds for the Minuteman III and Poseidon missiles, both assumed to be equipped with new MIRV (multiple, independently-targeted) warheads. Both missiles are included, even though there is a strong case for relying on Poseidon alone, thereby saving the $400 million a year that Minuteman III will cost by 1972. The decision to leave these controversial new weapons in the budget is based on the judgment that the U.S.S.R. is pushing ahead with the development of similar weapons, and that the arguments against them, while strong, are not conclusive. A successful outcome of the disarmament talks would, of course, allow cuts in spending on these weapons, while an accelerated build-up in the Soviet nuclear striking force conceivably could boost the post-Vietnam defense budget as high as $73 billion.

After the proposed cuts, the United States would still have the most powerful and diversified military force in the world; it would not be returning to a form of isolationism nor would it be in the position of carrying out unilateral disarmament. The analysis indicates that if many of the long-outdated assumptions in the defense field are questioned, sharp eyes and sharp pencils, in President Nixon's words, can produce a streamlined defense budget better suited to the realities of the 1970s.

HOW TO BREAK UP
THE MILITARY-INDUSTRIAL COMPLEX [7]

In 1963 the New York *Times* conducted a survey of the top twenty-five defense contractors and found that none of

[7] From *The Economy of Death*, by Richard J. Barnet, codirector of The Institute for Policy Studies, Washington, D.C. Atheneum. '69. p 144-59. Adapted from *The Economy of Death* by Richard J. Barnet. Copyright © 1969 by Richard J. Barnet. Reprinted by permission of Atheneum Publishers.

them had done any serious planning for conversion to non-defense production. Five years later Bernard Nossiter [of the Washington *Post*] found in a similar survey that the heads of defense firms, some of whom in the interim had experimented unsuccessfully with nonmilitary technology, had no intention of converting their plants to peace-oriented production. The major defense corporations have given no support to the efforts of Senator George McGovern [Democrat, South Dakota] and a few others in Congress who have tried to develop a Federal program to aid the conversion process. The presidents of the five largest defense contractors refused even to appear before Senator Proxmire's [Democrat, Wisconsin] Subcommittee on Economy in Government [of the Joint Economic Committee] to discuss how to end waste in the procurement process. Contractors derive too many advantages from military socialism to give it up easily. . . .

Defense contractors presently have no incentive to convert to the Economy of Life, and they do not believe they will ever have to do so. As long as the United States shares the planet with several billion neighbors, the supply of threats is inexhaustible. There is a weapons "revolution" every five years, a new piece of lethal technology that can always be sold. Despite recent attacks on the military, the weapons-makers do not see the political forces in America which will force a shift in national policy sufficient to require them to reorient their corporations. Until they do, they will take no initiative toward conversion, but will use their power to delay it.

Thus the entrenchment and concentration of economic and political power in the hands of the military-industrial complex is itself a prime obstacle to conversion. The public-relations and lobbying activities of the Pentagon play an important role in building and protecting that power. There is no legitimate reason for the armed forces to support over 6,000 public-relations men. . . . Congress should drastically cut the public-relations budget and prohibit the Pentagon from propagandizing the American people....

A strict conflict-of-interest law covering civilian and military personnel should be passed. The recruitment of top civilian officials of the Department of Defense from the defense industry should be prohibited, except in extraordinary cases. There are others available with equal talent and greater objectivity. Nor should military officers be able to count on retiring on an annuity from a defense contractor.

The Defense Department should be prohibited from contracting with universities for war research. Funds now disbursed by the Pentagon to universities for basic research in the physical and social sciences should be transferred to the National Science Foundation or some other civilian agency. War research corrupts the purposes and values of universities and renders the nation's institutions of learning dependent upon the military. If universities need Federal subsidies to survive, then the funds should be so labeled and made available from nonmilitary sources.

Essential research functions can be performed in in-house laboratories run by the Government on a fraction of the present military-research budget. About 80 per cent of the Pentagon's research activities, including research on chemical and germ warfare, war-game scenarios, and other refinements in the science of death is expendable....

The most critical aspect of the military-industrial complex is of course the relationship between the Pentagon and the top defense contractors. That relationship must be radically altered if the society is to move away from further militarization. It is not hard to see what is wrong with the relationship, but improvising solutions is difficult. There are two characteristics of industry's role in the defense process which are highly objectionable. The first is that a relatively few firms derive unfair economic advantages from what amounts to a public franchise. Such firms, which play so vital a role in setting national priorities, are public in every sense but one. They pocket substantial private profits, but are wholly unaccountable to the taxpayers who finance their operations.

The second objectionable feature is that the dependence of the defense industry on the Pentagon gives the military immense added power. It is not true that a few firms control the Pentagon and force it to foment wars to keep them in business. That is the straw-man theory of the military-industrial complex. The Pentagon's ability to control a major share of the nation's industrial production is the real problem, for it gives the Department of Defense a commanding position in the economy which carries with it a dangerous concentration of political power.

A traditional slogan of populist groups in America in earlier days was "Let's take the profits out of war." After World War I even the American Legion endorsed this principle. Recently J. K. Galbraith has proposed nationalizing any firm that does more than 75 per cent of its total business with the Defense Department. Taking the steam out of the weapons-pushing process by removing the profit incentive is an attractive notion. The conversion of a small number of absolutely essential defense plants into Government arsenals makes sense. Unfortunately, nationalization does not solve the more general problem of concentration of power. H. L. Nieburg [political scientist] of the University of Wisconsin has put the problem in what seems to me to be exactly the right light:

The old dichotomy between what is private and what is public is in the process of abandonment; but an explicit rubric which will protect democracy and the public interest has not been formulated. What must come is a system of values and institutions which will replace independence and pluralism. This task of formulation is the greatest challenge of the future. As economic pluralism disappears, only political pluralism, safeguarded by new institutions of representation, can make the exercise of power both responsive and limited. A heightened and more representative infrastructure of interest groups is necessary at all levels of society and may already be forming. The weakness of such interest groups in the past may have contributed to the use of R&D contracting as a form of indirect Government intervention in the economy. The problem is not as so many critics of the establishment believe, to control technology; rather, it is to control those interest groups and power coalitions who are—in the name of an automatic impersonal urge toward technological change—making public policy for the nation and holding in their hands much of the power of decision making for the whole society.

If General Dynamics became a Government agency, the Pentagon's accountability would not be automatically improved. There would still be no one representing the public interest to ask why the agency should be making a new weapon simply because it is technically feasible to do so. There would be no representative from the local community to point out that the addiction of the local economy to defense spending grows worse with the injection of each additional dollar. The problem of secrecy would remain and would probably be worse.

The hybrid public-private corporation is a major new phenomenon of American life extending far beyond the defense area. Its implications for American democracy are not understood. The congressional Conference on the Military Budget and National Priorities proposed the creation of a Temporary National Security Committee composed of members of Congress and private citizens to examine the institutional structure of the military-industrial establishment and to make recommendations to Congress. A principal task of such a committee should be to investigate the role of private corporations in setting public policy in the defense area and to propose legislation to subject such corporations to effective citizen control. A possible solution might be to have the public elect a certain percentage of the board of directors. The most important step is to reduce radically the flow of public funds into such companies.

*How to Give Up the Economy of Death
and Keep Prosperity*

When it comes to conversion, most Americans are Marxists. They do not believe that the present levels of prosperity or employment can be maintained except by a war economy. They do not see or will not admit the revolutionary implications of their belief. An economic system that works only by turning out products that endanger itself and the planet is literally suicidal. If it is true that American capitalism cannot function without military socialism, then anyone who cares about survival cannot be a capitalist. But is it true?

A central problem concerns unemployment. According to the University of California sociologist Jeffrey Schevitz, one in five jobs in the United States depends directly or indirectly upon the Department of Defense. The Pentagon has 3.4 million members in the armed forces and 1.3 million civilian workers spread across seventy countries. There are 3.8 million industrial workers whose lives are wholly tied to war production. Millions more are indirectly dependent upon the defense budget. Twenty-one per cent of skilled blue-collar workers are on military payrolls. Schevitz notes that nearly half of all scientists and engineers in private industry work in the aerospace and defense fields. . . .

What can the Federal Government do about unemployment once it is decided to convert the economy from war preparation? The question is central, for unless there is a program instead of platitudes for dealing with this problem, the resistance to conversion will be too strong to overcome.

A national conversion program should be established which operates on the basic principle that the community, not the individual war worker or soldier, must pay the costs of conversion. Like the GI Bill of Rights, such a program would ease the transition for persons whose jobs are destroyed as a result of Government policy. Government and a specialized industry have placed millions of workers in a position of dependence on the Economy of Death. They must now bear the responsibility for easing the pain of withdrawal.

Such a program should be administered by a National Conversion Commission with broad powers. A principal job of the commission would be to assist the retraining and relocation of people released from war research and war production. Under the Manpower and Development Training Act of 1962, limited funds are presently available for "brief refresher or reorientation educational courses in order to become qualified for other employment" to assist people "who have become unemployed because of the specialized nature of their former employment." This program in greatly expanded form should become a major instrument of conversion. In accordance with the national conversion plan, the commission should award substantial grants to scientific and technical personnel to encourage them to apply their talents to priority problems. The manpower specialist Herbert Striner of the Upjohn Institute estimates that it would take no more than three or four months to train most scientists and engineers now in war work for useful alternative jobs. For example, an engineer who specializes in the miniaturizing of electronic components for a missile might be given a Federal grant of up to a half-year's salary to study the technology of mass transportation, pollution, or low-cost housing. Another might be given a grant to design an experimental school. . . .

The same programs should be available for nonskilled workers. In some respects their problem is easier than that of the scientific and technical people. In others it is more difficult. Leonard A. Lecht of the National Planning Association estimates that if $20 billion were cut from the defense budget, half of which went to social programs and half into private profits through tax reduction, new job openings would exceed jobs lost through defense cutbacks by 325,000. But the new jobs would demand different skills—fewer machine operators and engineers, and more service personnel, craftsmen, and laborers to work in the building trades. The commission should have a nationwide program of job re-placement, retraining programs for unskilled workers, and the power to operate public-works programs with former defense workers.

The commission should adopt an explicit policy of min-imizing relocation to the greatest possible extent. Today it is common for workers laid off in one defense plant to move to a similar job in another city. However, some relocation will obviously be necessary, and the commission should have funds to purchase houses of defense workers who cannot otherwise sell them at a fair market price. It should also pay travel costs and other relocation expenses. Britain has had a comprehensive program since 1909 to help its workers re-locate to find suitable jobs. There should also be an income-maintenance program for defense workers to supplement normal unemployment benefits. Defense plants should be required to contribute to such a program by establishing insurance funds out of excess profits.

Communities that are dependent upon war industries or military installations should be eligible for special assis-tance. In a real sense they are "disaster areas" and should be eligible for the sort of extraordinary relief that is given to communities stricken by flood or tornado. When the Studebaker plant in South Bend, Indiana, closed in 1964, resulting in the layoff of 8,700 workers, a coordinated Fed-eral program of assistance was undertaken. However, the principal instrument used to rescue the community was the defense budget. The Department of Defense arranged for the sale of the Studebaker plant to other defense firms. The commission should stimulate nondefense production on a crash basis by making low-interest loans and emergency grants to affected communities. It could turn over federally owned military installations to the local community at nom-inal cost upon receipt of a community plan for the utiliza-tion of the property. In some cases an emergency negative income tax or other income-maintenance program would be necessary.

The costs of these and other programs that might be developed by the commission would be considerable, but they would be nowhere near the savings that could be realized by a substantial cut of the defense budget. Further, every dollar spent to stimulate useful production of goods and services needed to prevent social decay and to remove the injustices that lead to violence contributes to the real wealth of the nation as weapons stockpiles do not.

WE HAVE GOT TO GET RID OF NUCLEAR WEAPONS [8]

How real is the threat of full-scale nuclear war? I have my own very inexpert idea, but realizing how little I know and fearful that I may be a little paranoid on this subject, I take every opportunity to ask reputed experts. I asked that question of a very distinguished professor of government at Harvard about a month ago. I asked him what sort of odds he would lay on the possibility of full-scale nuclear war within the foreseeable future. "Oh," he said comfortably, "I think I can give you a pretty good answer to that question. I estimate the probability of full-scale nuclear war, provided that the situation remains about as it is now, at 2 per cent per year." Anybody can do the simple calculation that shows that 2 per cent per year means that the chance of having that full-scale nuclear war, by 1990 is about one in three, and by 2000 it is about 50-50. . . .

Perhaps you will think me altogether absurd, or "academic," or hopelessly innocent—that is, until you think of the alternatives—if I say as I do to you now: we have to get rid of those nuclear weapons. There is nothing worth having that can be obtained by nuclear war: nothing material or ideological, no tradition that it can defend. It is utterly self-defeating. Those atom bombs represent an unusable wea-

[8] From "Generation in Search of a Future," speech by George Wald, delivered at MIT, March 4, 1969. Text from *Representative American Speeches: 1968-1969*; ed. by Lester Thonssen. (Reference Shelf v 41 no 4) Wilson. '69. p 42-4. Dr. Wald is Higgins Professor of Biology at Harvard University and won the Nobel Prize in medicine and physiology in 1967.

pon. The only use for an atom bomb is to keep somebody else from using it. It can give us no protection, but only the doubtful satisfaction of retaliation. Nuclear weapons offer us nothing but a balance of terror; and a balance of terror is still terror.

We have to get rid of those atomic weapons, here and everywhere. We cannot live with them.

I think we've reached a point of great decision, not just for our nation, not only for all humanity, but for life upon the Earth. I tell my students, with a feeling of pride that I hope they will share, that the carbon, nitrogen and oxygen that makes up 99 per cent of our living substance, were cooked in the deep interiors of earlier generations of dying stars. Gathered up from the ends of the universe, over billions of years, eventually they came to form in part the substance of our sun, its planets and ourselves. Three billion years ago life arose upon the Earth. It is the only life in the solar system. Many a star has since been born and died.

About two million years ago, man appeared. He has become the dominant species on the Earth. All other living things, animal and plant, live by his sufferance. He is the custodian of life on Earth, and in the solar system. It's a big responsibility. The thought that we're in competition with Russians or with Chinese is all a mistake and trivial. We are one species, with a world to win. There's life all over this universe, but the only life in the solar system is on Earth; and in the whole universe, we are the only men.

Our business is with life, not death. Our challenge is to give what account we can of what becomes of life in the solar system, this corner of the universe that is our home and, most of all, what becomes of men—all men of all nations, colors and creeds. It has become one world, a world for all men. It is only such a world that now can offer us life and the chance to go on.

BIBLIOGRAPHY

An asterisk (*) preceding a reference indicates that the article or a part of it has been reprinted in this book.

BOOKS, PAMPHLETS, AND DOCUMENTS

Aron, Raymond. The great debate; theories of nuclear strategy. Doubleday. '65.

Aron, Raymond. On war. Doubleday. '59.

Art, R. J. The TFX decision: McNamara and the military. Little. '68.

Baar, James and Howard, W. E. Polaris! Harcourt. '60.

*Barnet, R. J. The economy of death. Atheneum. '69.

Baruch, Bernard. American industry in the war; ed. by R. H. Hippelheuser. Prentice-Hall. '41.

Batchelder, R. C. The irreversible decision, 1939-1950. Houghton. '62.

Berkowitz, Marvin. The conversion of military-oriented research and development to civilian uses. Praeger. '70.

Blow, Michael. The history of the atomic bomb; by the editors of American Heritage; consultant: W. W. Watson. American Heritage. '68.

Brennan, D. G. Arms control, disarmament and national security. Braziller. '61.

Christodoulou, A. P. Conversion of nuclear facilities from military to civilian uses: a case study in Hanford, Washington. Praeger. '70.

Compton, A. H. Atomic quest: a personal narrative. Oxford University Press. '56.

*Cook, F. J. The warfare state. Macmillan. '62; Collier. '64.

Cousins, Norman. In place of folly. Harper. '61.

Davis, E. H. Two minutes till midnight. Bobbs. '55.

*Davis, K. S. Experience of war: the United States in World War II. Doubleday. '65.

Dean, A. H. Test ban and disarmament: the path of negotiation. Harper (for the Council on Foreign Relations). '66.

De Seversky, A. P. America: too young to die. McGraw. '61.

Donovan, J. A. Jr. Militarism, USA. Scribner. '70.

Fulbright, J. W. The Pentagon propaganda machine. Liveright. '70.
  Excerpt. Saturday Review. 53:22-5+. N. 7, '70. Governance of the Pentagon.

*Galbraith, J. K. How to control the military. Doubleday; paper ed. New American Library. '69.
  Same. Harper's Magazine. 238:31-46. Je. '69.

Green, Philip. Deadly logic: the theory of nuclear deterrence. Ohio State University Press. '66.
  Review. Bulletin of the Atomic Scientists. 24:24-7. F. '68. M. H. Armacost.

Groueff, Stéphane. Manhattan project: the untold story of the making of the atomic bomb. Little. '67.

Groves, L. R. Now it can be told: the story of the Manhattan project. Harper. '62.

Howard, Michael. Studies in war and peace. Viking. '70.

Kahn, Herman. On thermonuclear war. Princeton University Press. '60.

Kissinger, H. A. Nuclear weapons and foreign policy. Harper (for the Council on Foreign Relations). '57.

Knebel, Fletcher and Bailey, C. W. 2d. No high ground. Harper. '60.

Kolko, Gabriel. Politics of war: the world & United States foreign policy, 1943-45. Random House. '70.

*Lapp, R. E. Arms beyond doubt. Cowles. '70.

Lapp, R. E. Atoms and people. Harper. '56.

Le May, C. E. and Smith, D. O. America is in danger. Funk & Wagnalls. '68.
  Excerpts. U.S. News & World Report. 64:14. Je. 10, '68. Le May warns: U.S. faces grave danger.

*Lens, Sidney. The military-industrial complex. Pilgrim. '70.

Lynch, J. E. Local economic development after military base closures. Praeger. '70.

Mack-Forlist, D. M. and Newman, Arthur. The conversion of ship-building from military to civilian markets. Praeger. '70.

McNamara, R. S. The essence of security: reflections in office. Harper. '68.

Melman, Seymour, ed. The defense economy: conversion of industries and occupations to civilian needs. Praeger. '70.

*Melman, Seymour. Pentagon capitalism: the political economy of war. McGraw. '70.
  Review. Nation. 211:182-4. S. 7, '70. R. F. Kaufman.

Mollenhoff, Clark. The Pentagon: politics, profits and plunder. Putnam. '67.

Murray, T. E. Nuclear policy for war and peace. World. '60.

Nieburg, H. L. In the name of science. Quadrangle. '66.

Polmar, Norman. Atomic submarines. Van Nostrand. '63.

Power, T. S. Design for survival. Coward-McCann. '65.

Proxmire, William. Report from wasteland: America's military-industrial complex. Praeger. '70.
  Review. Saturday Review. 53:29-31+. Ap. 25, '70. Eliot Janeway.

Russell, Bertrand. Common sense and nuclear warfare. Simon & Schuster. '59.

Schelling, T. C. and Halperin, M. H. Strategy and arms control. Twentieth Century Fund. '61.

*Scoville, Herbert, and Osborn, R. C. Missile madness. Houghton. '70.

Stanley, D. T. and others. Men who govern: a biographical profile of Federal political executives. Brookings. '67.

Teller, Edward and Latter, A. L. Our nuclear future: facts, dangers, and opportunities. Criterion. '58.

Thayer, George. The war business: the international trade in armaments. Simon & Schuster. '69.

*Twining, N. F. Neither liberty nor safety. Holt. '66.

Tyrrell, C. M. Pentagon partners, the new nobility. Grossman. '70.

Ullman, J. E. ed. Potential civilian markets for the military-electronics industry: strategies for conversion. Praeger. '70.

Waskow, A. I. ed. The debate over thermonuclear strategy. Heath. '65.

Wilson, T. W. Jr. The great weapons heresy. Houghton. '70.

Yale, Wesley and others. Alternative to armageddon. Rutgers University Press. '70.

Yarmolinsky, Adam. The military establishment: its impacts on American society. Harper. '71.

PERIODICALS

Annals of the American Academy of Political and Social Science. 78:1-227. '18. Mobilizing America's resources for the war; ed. by Carl Kelsey.

Atlantic. 221:89-94. Je. '68. Two cents and more: advice to the secretary of defense; symposium.

Atlantic. 223:51-6. Ap. '69. The new American militarism. D. M. Shoup and J. A. Donovan.

Aviation Week & Space Technology. 86:32-3. Ap. 24, '67. DOD [Department of Defense], industry clash on support awards. D. C. Winston.

Aviation Week & Space Technology. 88:19-21. F. 12, '68. Force-level cuts planned to trim defense spending.

Aviation Week & Space Technology. 88:69-75. Mr. 18, '68. Dollar drain saps U.S. strategic stance. Cecil Brownlow.

Aviation Week & Space Technology. 89:19. Jl. 29, '68. House unit votes $72.2 billion for DOD [Department of Defense], expects supplemental. Katherine Johnsen.

Aviation Week & Space Technology. 89:14. D. 16, '68. $4 billion DOD [Department of Defense] supplemental seen. Cecil Brownlow.

Aviation Week & Space Technology. 90:34. Ap. 14, '69. Grumman fights excess Viet profits case. Katherine Johnsen.

Aviation Week & Space Technology. 90:16-18. Je. 30, '69. Initial overrun review completed. Cecil Brownlow.

Aviation Week & Space Technology. 90:47+. Je. 30, '69; 92:55. Ja. 12, '70. NASA lists top 100 contractors.

Aviation Week & Space Technology. 91:21. O. 6, '69. DOD fights expanded authority for GAO. Katherine Johnsen.

Aviation Week & Space Technology. 91:104-5+. N. 17, '69. Defense department lists leading 100 contractors for fiscal 1969.

Bulletin of the Atomic Scientists. 25:10-17. Ap. '69. Forces affecting science policy; R&D address, August 30, 1968. D. E. Kash.

Bulletin of the Atomic Scientists. 25:38+. Ap. '69. Military complex: the unpleasant symptom. J. C. Dougherty.

Business Week. p 122-4+. Jl. 16, '66. Putting a dollar sign on everything.

Business Week. p 112+. F. 15, '69. Critics fire at military budget.

Business Week. p 35. Je. 7, '69. Lockheed's ledger on the C-5A.

Business Week. p 68-71. Je. 7, '69. Can defense work keep a home on the campus?

Business Week. p 20. Ag. 6, '69. After ABM, weapons are still targets.

Business Week. p 140. O. 25, '69. Military markets start to sag.

Business Week. p 130. N. 8, '69. Who pulled in the big ones?

Business Week. p 91+. D. 6, '69. Military cutbacks will send tremors through industry; forecast for the 1970's.

Business Week. p 64. Ag. 1, '70. The experts plan a new Pentagon.

Commonweal. 89:380-1. D. 13, '68. Swords, plowshares and PR. Amitai Etzioni.

Commonweal. 90:58. Ap. 4, '69. News and views: L. M. Rivers and defense contracts. John Deedy.

Commonweal. 90:156-7. Ap. 25, '69. Disarming the Pentagon.

Commonweal. 90:252-3. My. 16, '69. Auditing the Pentagon.

Commonweal. 91:273-6. N. 28, '69. How to cut the military budget by $54 billion. Seymour Melman.

*Congressional Record. 110 (daily) :7093-7. Ap. 7, '64. The cold war in American life; address delivered at University of North Carolina, Chapel Hill, April 5, 1964. J. W. Fulbright.
        Same. Vital Speeches of the Day. 30:422-7. My. 1, '64.

*Congressional Record. 115 (daily) :5699-704. Mr. 10, '69. Blank check for the military; address before U.S. Senate, March 10, 1969. William Proxmire.
        Same. Vital Speeches of the Day. 35:400-5. Ap. 15, '69.

*Congressional Record. 115 (daily) :9127-31. Ap. 15, '69. The military-industrial complex. Barry Goldwater.
    Same abridged with title: Why a "military-industrial complex"?—a senator's answer. U.S. News & World Report. 66:88-90. Ap. 28, '69.
Current. 100:64. O. '68. Arms politics: the state of the art. Clayton Fritchey.
*Department of State Bulletin. 44:179-82. F. 6, '61. Farewell radio and television address to the American people, January 17, 1961. D. D. Eisenhower.
Electronic News. 14:21. Je. 2, '69. Betts defends military-industry team. Bruce Le Boss.
Electronic News. 15:28. Ja. 19, 70. Watch out for the watchdog [General Accounting Office]. Jack Robertson.
Esquire. 73:66B+. Ja. '70. At play with the military-industrial complex. Paul Dickson and Robert Skole.
*Fortune. 80:68-73+. Ag. 1, '69. The case for cutting defense spending. Juan Cameron.
Fortune. 80:74-5. Ag. 1, '69. Where the military contracts go]with charts]. W. S. Rukeyser.
Fortune. 80:82-3+. Ag. 1, '69. Defense profits: the hidden issue. A. T. Demaree.
Fortune. 80:84-7+. Ag. 1, '69. Military-industrial complex, Russian style. Richard Armstrong.
Fortune. 80:43+. D. '69. Demands for cuts in the defense budget have led to a fundamental change in our global strategy. Juan Cameron.
Fortune. 82:110-13. S. '70. Making the turn to a peacetime economy; recession in defense-related industries. Sanford Rose.
Harper's Magazine. 242:37-40+. F. '71. The programming of Robert McNamara. David Halberstam.
Harvard Business Review. 45:111-23. Jl. '67. Price of admission into the defense business. Martin Meyerson.
Harvard Business Review. 46:53-64. My. '68. Growing threat of our military-industrial complex. Jack Raymond.
Harvard Business Review. 47:146-55. My. '69. Let's internationalize defense marketing. R. E. McGarrah.
Harvard Business Review. 47:90-8. Jl. '69. Handling risk in defense contracting. R. M. Anderson.
Harvard Business Review. 47:162-4+. N. '69. Anguish in the defense industry. R. M. Anderson.
Iron Age. 204:73. Jl. 31, '70. Military complex suffers message gap. D. N. Williams.
*Journal of American History. 56:819-39. Mr. '70. The "industrial-military complex" in historical perspective: the interwar years. P. A. C. Koistinen.

Look. 33:13-28+. Ag. 12; 17-24. Ag. 26, '69. American militarism.

Look. 33:28-9. Ag. 26, '69. Defense contract; the money web. Gerald Astor.

Monthly Labor Review. 92:21-5. Je. '69. Skill transfers; can defense workers adapt to civilian occupations? J. R. Cambern and D. A. Newton.

Nation. 205:686-9. D. 25, '67. Feast at the Pentagon. Sanford Watzman.

Nation. 207:100-1. Ag. 19, '68. Undiscussed issue; defense budget vs. funds for the cities.

Nation. 207:355-6. O. 14, '68. Pentagon speaks; scientists opposed to Vietnamese war rebuked.

Nation. 207:386. O. 21, '68. Military supermarket.

Nation. 207:684-6. D. 23, '68. Pentagon loot. R. G. Sherrill.

Nation. 208:354. Mr. 24, '69. Key issue: military demands vs. civilian needs.

Nation. 208:525. Ap. 28, '69. Place in history: accredited to Dwight Eisenhower.

Nation. 209:36-7. Jl. 14, '69. Contempt of Congress.

Nation. 209:197. S. 8, '69. Real trouble for the Pentagon.

Nation. 210:484-5. Ap. 27, '70. Angry old man. George Wald.

National Observer. p 3. Ag. 3, '70. Panel urges overhaul of Pentagon. J. G. Driscoll.

National Review. 20:1213+. D. 3, '68. Decentralizing the Pentagon. Anthony Harrigan.

*National Review. 22:1110. O. 20, '70. In the McNamara vein. Anthony Harrigan.

New Republic. 159:26-8. S. 28, '68. Cutting the defense budget. R. E. Lapp.

New Republic. 160:10-11. My. 10, '69. Managed propaganda, condoned disorder? John Osborne.

New Republic. 161:15-18. D. 20, '69. Myth of war profiteering. G. E. Berkley.

New Republic. 162:22-4. Ap. 25, '70. End to concealment. P. H. Douglas.

*New Republic. 163:19-23. Ag 1, '70. The Lockheed scandal. J. G. Phillips.

*New Republic. 163:16-20. Ag. 22-29, '70. Cutting the Pentagon down to size. R. E. Lapp.

New Republic. 164:7-8. F. 6, '71. Pentagon power.

*New York Review of Books. p 5-6. Jl. 23, '70. Military America. R. L. Heilbroner.
    Essay on Pentagon capitalism, by Seymour Melman.

New York Times. p 12. My. 27, '70. Senate panel backs curb on Pentagon. R. M. Smith.

New York Times. p 27. D. 29, '70. O what a lovely Pentagon. Herbert Mitgang.

New York Times. p 13. Ja. 5, '71. Congressmen told of $693-million arms sales under Food for Peace program. J. W. Finney.

New York Times. p 1+. Ja. 21, '71. Foreign policy: Pentagon also encounters rebuffs. William Beecher.

New York Times. p 1+. Ja. 27, '71. Impasse reported on Lockheed cost. Neil Sheehan.

New York Times. p 1+. F. 2, '71. Lockheed accepts a loss of $200-million on C-5A. Neil Sheehan.

New York Times. p 1+. F. 8, '71. U.S. agency finds huge arms waste.

New York Times. p 33. F. 8; p 39. F. 9, '71. The problem of MIRV. Herbert Scoville.

New York Times Magazine. p 15+. My. 17, '64. Strangelove? R. L. Gilpatric.

*New York Times Magazine. p 10-11+. Je. 22, '69. As Eisenhower was saying . . . "We must guard against unwarranted influence by the military-industrial complex." R. F. Kaufman.

New York Times Magazine. p 30-1+. O. 19, '69. Antimilitarism can be too much of a good thing. Anthony Hartley.

New York Times Magazine. p 50-1+. N. 16, '69. Big defense firms are really public firms. J. K. Galbraith.

Newsweek. 62:72. Jl. 1, '63. Irreparable loss: civilian authority. Raymond Moley.

Newsweek. 73:32. Mr. 31, '69. M-I complex. Kenneth Crawford.

Newsweek. 73:29-30+. Je. 2, '69. Antimilitary complex.

Newsweek. 73:71-2. Je. 2, '69. Crisis at Lockheed.

Newsweek. 73:74-6+. Je. 9, '69. Military-industrial complex.

Newsweek. 73:81. Je. 9, '69. Arms and the market. Clem Morgello.

Newsweek. 75:87+. Mr. 16, '70. Partner in trouble.

Newsweek. 76:53-4. Ag. 10, '70. Defense's "Fly before you buy" policy.

Reader's Digest. 95:54-8. Ag. '69. New alarm; the submarine gap. F. V. Drake.

Reporter. 35:29-31. D. 1, '66. High cost of not spending; concerning hearings on the Pentagon's cost-reduction program savings claims. J. L. Brooks.

Reporter. 38:15-18. Ap. 18, '68. How the military rate McNamara's performance. H. W. Baldwin.

Saturday Review. 51:30-4. Mr. 16, '68. What is power doing to the Pentagon? Marvin Kalb.

Saturday Review. 51:8-10+. D. 21, '68. Pursuit of military security; the power of the Pentagon. E. J. McCarthy.

Saturday Review. 53:14-17. Ja. 31, '70. Pentagon vs. free enterprise. William Proxmire.

Science. 138:797-8. N. 16, '62. Who runs America? an examination
of a theory that says the answer is a military-industrial complex. D. S. Greenberg.
    Discussion. Science. 139:247-8+. Ja 18, '63.

Science. 160:400-2. Ap. 26, '68. Defense research; Senate critics
urge redeployment to urban needs. D. S. Greenberg.

Science. 161:446-8. Ag. 2, '68. Research probe: Rickover broad-
sides military-scientific complex.

Science News. 93:315-16. Mr. 30, '68. Attacking the weapons
culture. Carl Behrens.

Senior Scholastic. 95:3-7+. N. 10, '69. Military-industrial complex,
mountain or molehill?

Time. 91:21-2. My. 3, '68. McNamara's legacy; long-range defense
planning.

Time. 91:13-14. My. 31, '68. Warfare by witchcraft; questioning
the Pentagon's military-science research programs.

Time. 93:20-4+. Ap. 11, '69. Military: servant or master of policy?
    Same abridged. Reader's Digest. 95:235-6+. Jl. '69. U.S. military:
    servant or master?

Time. 93:23. Ap. 11, '69. What is the military-industrial complex?

Time. 93:76-7. My. 30, '69. Lockheed's casualties in the defense
controversy.

Time. 94:16-17. Je. 11, '69. Pentagon purgatory; committee to
review management, research, procurement and decision-making operations.

Time. 96:8-10. Ag. 10, '70. Shaping the amorphous lump [dis-
cussion of the Fitzhugh report].

Trans-Action. 5:29-38. My. '68. Social science yogis and military
commissars. I. L. Horowitz.

U.S. News & World Report. 65:28. Jl. 15, '68. Why Joint Chiefs
worry over U.S. survival; excerpts from Senate hearing. E. G.
Wheeler.

U.S. News & World Report. 65:16. S. 30, '68. Noted admiral
looks inside Pentagon and tells what's wrong; excerpts from
testimony. H. G. Rickover.

U.S. News & World Report. 65:19. O. 7, '68. Solve U.S. domestic
ills with defense billions? that's Clifford's new idea.

U.S. News & World Report. 65:14-15. O. 14, '68. Is U.S. neglecting
its defenses, inviting aggression, disaster? excerpts from statement by R. B. Russell.

U.S. News & World Report. 66:6 Ja. 27, '69. U.S. posture, Clifford's size-up; excerpts from statement January 18, 1969.
C. M. Clifford.

U.S. News & World Report. 66:100. My. 12, '69. Gambling with the security of the American people. David Lawrence.

U.S. News & World Report. 66:14. Je. 9, '69. Top general's rebuttal to attacks on military; excerpts from address, May 17, 1969. E. G. Wheeler.

U.S. News & World Report. 66:16. Je. 23, '69. Witch hunt against the military? A warning; excerpts from statement to a subcommittee of the Joint Economic Committee of Congress, June 11, 1969. Dean Acheson.

U.S. News & World Report. 67:30-2. S. 8, '69. Defense under fire; the reason.

U.S. News & World Report. 68:7. Ja. 12, '70. On the warpath over arms costs.

*U.S. News & World Report. 68:34-9. Ap. 20, '70. Why defense planners worry; interview. E. G. Wheeler.

U.S. News & World Report. 69:24-6+. N. 30, '70. Russia vs. U.S.: coming crisis in arms; interview. J. S. Foster, Jr.

Vital Speeches of the Day. 34:354-8. Ap. 1, '68. Realities of military preparedness; address, February 26, 1968. Strom Thurmond.

*Vital Speeches of the Day. 35:410-13. Ap. 15, '69. Generation in search of a future; address delivered at MIT, March 4, 1969. George Wald.

    Same with title: Our business is with life. Redbook. 133:68. Ag. '69; *Excerpts.* New Yorker. 45:29-31. Mr. 22, '69.

Vital Speeches of the Day. 35:455-60. My. 15, '69. Militarism and the American democracy; address, April 8, 1969. J. W. Fulbright.

*Vital Speeches of the Day. 35:460-2. My. 15, '69. Defense requirements for the 1970's; address before AFCEA [Armed Forces Communications and Electronics Association], April 3, 1969. J. J. Rhodes.

*Vital Speeches of the Day. 35:523-8. Je. 15, '69. Military-industrial complex; address presented to 14th Annual Institute of World Affairs at Washington State University, Pullman, Washington, March 21, 1969. M. L. Weidenbaum.

Vital Speeches of the Day. 36:93-6. N. 15, '69. Adequate defense; address, October 4, 1969. J. W. Carpenter 3d.

*Vital Speeches of the Day. 36:655-8. Ag. 15, '70. Assault on American industry; address before Commonwealth Club, San Francisco, July 10, 1970. Robert Anderson.

*Vital Speeches of the Day. 36:701-4. S. 1, '70. Some concerns about national security; address delivered before Air War College graduating class, June 5, 1970. I. C. Eaker.